Don't Think of a Blue Ball is as simple or as complicated as you want it to be, depending on how P[...] It aims to give you all you [...] and be joyful as you pursu[...] and do the effective, tried [...] Malti Bhojwani's extensive study and hours of co[...] clients. This book includes scientific explanations where needed, wisdom from timeless philosophers and authors, teachings from the scriptures together with the author's own personal poignant experiences to beautifully illustrate how you too can live a life you desire instead of one of default.

For the first time, an easy to read book that entwines humour, simple analogies and a firm voice in twelve chapters to show you how to make lasting changes in all areas of your life by making empowering decisions that will instantly help you experience joyous living.

You will not only learn how to take action towards your desired life by following steps like in many other self-help books, but also how to change the way you talk to yourself, enabling you to feel, walk and dream in a state that will magnetise everything you desire even while you sleep.

Don't Think of a Blue Ball will help you become aware of who you are being twenty-four hours a day and how to create a successful life by being a manifesting body that radiates joy and gratitude.

Don't Think of a BLUE BALL

Malti Bhojwani

Om Books International

First published in 2012 by

Om Books International

Corporate & Editorial Office
A-12, Sector 64, Noida 201 301
Uttar Pradesh, India
Phone: +91 120 477 4100
Email: editorial@ombooks.com
Website: www.ombooksinternational.com

Sales Office
4379/4B, Prakash House, Ansari Road
Darya Ganj, New Delhi 110 002, India
Phone: +91 11 2326 3363, 2326 5303
Fax: +91 11 2327 8091
Email: sales@ombooks.com
Website: www.ombooks.com

Text copyright © Malti Bhojwani, 2012

All rights reserved. No part of this book may be reproduced or transmitted in any form by any means, electronic or mechanical, including photocopying and recording, or by any information storage and retrieval system, except as may be expressly permitted in writing by the publisher.

ISBN: 978-93-81607-15-2

10 9 8 7 6 5 4 3 2 1

Printed in India

For Drishti...

Contents

Introduction   *9*

Chapter-1
Ending Your Life as You Know It   **13**
The first chapter looks at the patterns you have been repeating and therefore getting the same results, over and over. By looking at the results, you can refocus on desired results. The entire world will be richer when you achieve your desires.

Chapter-2
Plugging In to Source   **26**
You are not alone. There is a higher purpose and energy involved in your manifestations. Learn how to Plug In to it and notice when you are not plugged.

Chapter-3
Making it Public   **46**
The power of deciding and then declaring. Jigsaw Puzzle Visualisation Exercise using NLP techniques to see the desired outcome and reinforce trust.

Chapter-4
Moving Forward   **66**
Take the first steps even when you are not sure how to proceed and trust your inner navigational system.

Chapter-5
Replacing Negativity   **78**
Stories we tell ourselves can create limiting beliefs that present obstacles in being able to have what we want. Change the stories and change your outcome. You can't unthink if you haven't already thought of a Blue Ball.

Chapter-6
Walking on Sunshine
106

When you say No to something, you are saying Yes to something else. Just like how a hot-air balloon navigates through the sky by riding the direction of the wind, sometimes you, too, have to stop doing and start allowing.

Chapter-7
Letting Go
126

We make the best choice based on the available alternatives at the time. Forgiveness is the only way to freedom.

Chapter-8
Coincidences and Intuition
145

Trust your intuition and learn to hone your ability to know. Synchronicity and coincidences are everywhere, you can either live like everything is randomly unrelated, or you can see the magic.

Chapter-9
Love
156

It is only when we become aware of all the love already around us that we can be open to more. Love is compassion, you have to be open to feeling, to love and be loved. Placing your relationship 'order' with the Universe and how to nurture your relationships.

Chapter-10
Wealth and Health
183

Acknowledge the wealth you already have, trust that you are just an instrument of the Universe's limitless opulence and supply. Do your work, and focus on the value you are giving out in order to feel healthy and be wealthy.

Chapter-11
Gratitude
210

Having an attitude of gratitude and appreciation will lead to more to be grateful for. Allow people to give to you as well and be willing to ask for help.

Chapter-12
The Beginning of the Rest of Your Life
223

Piece it al together and put it all into practice. It is about practicing new habits and ensuring that you are doing and thinking every single day thoughts that will bring you closer and closer to what you desire.

Acknowledgements— A Few Pages From My TAG Journal   230

Introduction

Standing on the porch on a crisp Wednesday morning, I shut my eyes as a gentle gust of wind caressed my cheeks. The scent of fresh rain still hung in the air as I inhaled deeply and smiled. Dressed in my tracksuit I was waiting to be picked up for my Pilates class, and at that moment I could not help but marvel at my creation, for I was living the life I had always dreamt.

It all started in November 2008 after a conversation with my dear friend and fellow author Chandru Bhojwani, who pepped me up to start the manifestation process. Approaching mid-month, I walked into the office where I had worked for 3 years and confronted not only my boss but also the fear that prevented me from attaining the life I wanted. My boss at the time, Yaron, was a good man; a man I respected and adored but I wanted the life I believed I deserved and after describing it to him, I quit.

I had trained to be a life coach many years ago and practiced it only part time, as I did not have the belief that I could succeed. I had 'safety-nets' all over the place, in case I could not make a living as a coach. These 'safety-nets' prevented me from succeeding. When I described my passion and vision to be a full-time coach and writer to my boss he, too, saw why I had to leave the job.

It was daunting and sometimes overwhelming, making me wonder and even question my decision at first but friends and family provided help and support in every way. Everything started to fall into place and six months later, I was working from home. Being able to create a comfortable and nurturing space for my daughter while she studied for her class 12 exams, hitting the gym twice a day, I finally had the chance to touch the lives of others through my work every day.

Being a single mother financial security was a concern but the strangest thing started to happen, I began to attract money. Whether it was 5 cents on the floor of car parks, or friends and well-wishers who had faith in me sponsoring projects worth thousands of dollars, the Universe was providing.

Today, I have lost weight and am the slimmest I have ever been, I am feeling more loved than I have ever felt and I have always wanted to be a published writer and here you are holding this book in your hands. I *did* and *will* continue to manifest my desires, as you will.

Trust that this book has landed in your hands at the time you are ready to fly and take-off. This will not be the last book that will help you harness your personal power, in fact after reading this book you will notice that your hunger for personal development will grow manifold. The learning will never end. Read with an open mind and practice straight away.

The most common mistake we commit is to procrastinate our development even when a book like this hits us on the head. Start today, the longer you take the less likely you are to do it. Don't let this be just another book you read, and put away; my invitation to you is to do the exercises and practices at the end of each chapter and declare your desires and intentions to someone, a friend, a coach or even on your social networking profile to help you keep yourself accountable. Why don't you go ahead and tell *everybody* about *that* thing in your mind. Tell them! *NOW!*

Set reminders on your phone and calendar to ensure action. When you put these steps in place, you will create a harness to make sure that you will not be able to fall too far down while you go up and scale your mountains.

I

Ending Your Life as You Know It

Every new beginning comes from some other beginning's end.
— *Seneca*

Like the Law of Gravity, the Law of Attraction is always in play and at any given moment, we are creating and manifesting. You may not be aware of it and believe it does not apply to you. However, just as you would not throw this book out of the window, as it will inevitably fall, ignoring the Law of Attraction also has its consequences.

The life you have led until this moment—the good, the bad and the ugly—is *your* creation. It is the sum total of *your* thoughts and wants that have brought you to this very moment of your life. The Universe has been eavesdropping on the thoughts of your inner soul and has been providing what it feels you desire. The principle behind the Law of Attraction is simple, *what you focus on is what you will attract into your life*. If you want to know what you have been drawing into your life, just look at your living environment, the people who surround you, the interactions you have with these people, your financial state of affairs, your fitness etc. Note your focus and note the energies that surround that focus. Maybe you managed to finally get a date with that girl you had a crush on for weeks, or perhaps your husband finally bought you that diamond pendant you were eying in the jewellery store, or that business deal you were anticipating came through. These are the areas, then, that you have definitely been focusing on and vibrating positive energies in. The flipside is true, too, with negative thinking creating negative energies, resulting in undesired results.

I was visiting my family in India and on a Sunday afternoon, this is when I was still living in Australia, I woke up from a nap and mum decided to brew some tea. Many thoughts crossed my mind and as my mother and I shared tea and biscuits, she identified that we often discuss the same topics. I was always complaining about how I had no time to cook, how I had put on weight, my clothes were tight, my daughter was always falling sick, my lower back ached, even my work colleagues were rude to me. In light of the Law of Attraction, it is not surprising that on this afternoon with my mother I had even more problems and negativity to report than usual. This time it was speeding tickets, debt collection letters, nasty comments from colleagues, accidents and inappropriate attention from the wrong men. The more I told my collection of 'sad stories' and repeated the incidents to the people in my life, the more they perpetuated. I was focusing on all the things that were wrong about my life and how these could not get any worse, but without realising, it was this thinking that attracted more of the same disappointment. The more I complained, the more I had to complain about. I sounded like a broken record and had become my own worst companion. 'I' was the problem. I was manifesting all the troubles in my life. Does it sound familiar?

It was at that moment I decided to make a positive change in my life. I examined my life from top to bottom, from my living space and the emails I send and receive to my conversations and friendships. What I had around me was a direct reflection of what I had been focusing on and, therefore, what I was *attracting*. I made a mental note each time I caught myself complaining or being negative. Once I had identified all my problem areas, I could concentrate on the cure.

Everything you already have in your life is a direct reflection of what you have focused *on*, thought *of* and vibrated *out*. So just as you do not even realise how you managed to create so many undesirable outcomes, because it was so effortless and easy on your part, you *can* consciously change your thoughts, focus and vibrations and hence change the results you see in your world. You were manifesting all the time.

What does manifesting mean? Merriam-Webster defines 'manifest' as:

\# readily perceived by the senses and especially by the sense of sight;

\# easily understood or recognised by the mind: obvious.

Trust that what you want is already there in the spiritual realm, just that we mortals in the physical world/sphere are yet to experience it! In order to see, you have to have faith and you have to believe that your energies and positive expectations will uncover the veil and reveal it to you.

Change your focus. Refocus on the desired results

Once you acknowledge how easy it is to attract factors in your life that you do not want and accept how effective and simple the law is, you can start using it to your advantage.

We have desires and wishes. After all, we are only human. My desire was to own a convertible and I knew exactly the make and model I wanted. Like a teenage girl infatuated with a boy-band, I printed pictures of it and pasted them on my walls at home and at work. When driving around the streets of Sydney, I could spot it from a mile away just by an inch of its body that jutted around the corner. The fact is, when you truly desire something, you will recognise it always. It is as if the radar in your mind switches to high alert for that particular thing and when it is within proximity the sirens go off. A few months later, I found myself hovering over that convertible, confused if I should pick the black or the red. I ended picking the black car with red leather interior. Whenever I punched the accelerator and felt the wind blow through my hair, I thought of my ability and never to doubt my manifesting powers.

Many of us find it difficult to veer away from the negative, which is understandable. If it is happening in reality how can you not think or talk about it? A good analogy for this issue is how we handle the headlights of oncoming traffic when driving at night. Why are we told to not look at the oncoming traffic's headlights? It is simple. If we let our attention wander to the light, we may, due to a natural tendency, veer our steering wheel towards the light and face a head-on collision with oncoming traffic. Hardly a desired outcome! But the madness is that we do the same in our daily lives when charting a course for ourselves. Like those lights, you know the problems of your life are waiting for a head-on collision, but the focus should be on the road ahead. Like everything in life, those lights will eventually pass you by and all that will remain is the highway and the possibilities of the journey ahead. What you focus on is what you will head towards, and create for yourself to experience.

It may not be positive to focus on what you don't want, but in this book we will ask you to look there just once in a while. Identifying and analysing what you don't want is one of the easiest ways to identify what it is you *do* desire to have in your life. These desires can become the focus of your thoughts and you will be well on your way to creating the life of your dreams.

Don't wants!

Identifying your 'don't wants' to help see your 'wants'.

These are the facets of your life that you want to get far away from because of how unpleasant they make you feel. Like a dark cloud they hover above, or perhaps it is that uneasy feeling in the back of our mind we struggle to escape. The causal factor could be just one thing, or perhaps an amalgamation of reasons. Once aware of the symptoms, like a doctor we must identify the cause before we find the cure. Let us consider the following examples to picture it better.

John, a thirty-two-year-old male client, had expressed a nagging feeling of emptiness that kept resurfacing. During working hours and social outings he managed to escape the sensation but when he was alone, it returned and led to a sense of depression. As a result, he buried himself with work and increased social activity to try to escape the emotion, only to have it return with a higher intensity. He realised his soul was communicating to him and no matter how much he tried, there was no escape from the truth within. But once he tried to analyse the root of the emotion, he began to express the issues he had and wanted to change.

'I am tired of the meaningless flings and waking up with hangovers all the time. I used to enjoy the attention and the feeling of conquest but it all feels empty now. And I cannot help feel that most of my friends take advantage of me and they don't appreciate or value my friendship.'

What did John want?

He wanted to be in a committed relationship with one woman whose company he enjoyed so much that he would not need to drink himself under the table, while out with his mates trying to 'pick-up'. He wanted to be surrounded by true friends who gave as much as they took in their friendships with him.

Natalie, a twenty-eight-year-old woman, expressed that she no longer wanted to sit around waiting for the phone to beep or ring every time she met a new guy, wondering if he liked her or not. She did not want to be scared every morning because her boss might ask her a question she didn't have the answer for, and she did not want always to have to check the prices in the menu before ordering her food. Plus she did not want to wear tatty shoes till they were worn out before being able to justify buying new ones. She was tired of always being broke.

What did Natalie want?

One need not be an expert to understand what she wanted. It can be as simple as looking for the polar opposite of what she did not want. When you don't want to be single, you want to be in a loving and committed relationship. When you don't want to be afraid, you want to feel strong and confident. When you don't want to be broke, you want to have abundance of wealth in your life.

When we take a moment to identify the 'don't wants' that we say and think habitually, we gain true insight into what our heart desires and are so much closer to achieving the life we want. A good exercise for you is to try to list your don't wants, consider the opposite of these negative desires by turning them into wants and you will discover what you truly desire.

Take a piece of paper and divide it into half. On the left column you will list ten of your 'don't wants'. Referring to the list on the left, you will fill in the right half of the paper with the opposite desires.

First list the 'don't wants', such as:
I don't want to go out with a smoker.
I don't want to live in this city all my life.
I don't want to be renting forever.
I don't want to receive another bill.
I don't want to be late.
I don't want to be dominated or controlled.
I don't want to fall sick so often.

Now that you have your 'don't wants' on the left side, you can easily fill up the right side with your wants.

Don't Wants	Wants
# I don't want to go out with a smoker	# I want a relationship with someone who is health-conscious
# I don't want to live in this city all my life	# I want the freedom to move with peace of mind
# I don't want to be renting forever	# I want to be a homeowner
# I don't want to receive another bill	# I want to have positive outstanding credit with my amenities' providers
# I don't want to be late	# I want to be punctual
# I don't want to be dominated or controlled.	# I want to be independent and appreciated for it
# I don't want to fall sick so often	# I want to be healthy

Once you have your 'wants' list—and don't worry you can always add to it as we run along—you are ready for the rest of this book. You will be on your way to manifesting your heart's desires.

Remember, too, that just because you are listing only ten 'wants' today, you can have many many more. You can have it all—as long as they are congruent, and as long as you realise that your practice to manifest your desires and setting your balloon off into the skies will in the process help manifest the desires of countless other people in your life.

It is important that you understand congruency here.

Congruency is wanting things that are parallel to each other and not contradictory.

You cannot simultaneously want to eat a chocolate cake everyday in front of the TV and want to be slim. You cannot want to be single and carefree and want to be in a loving, exclusive relationship.

Now that you have a list of congruent wants, look at the feelings that having these wants will give you.

John wants:
\# To be in a committed relationship
\# To feel loved, cared for and significant

When he thinks of being in this woman's embrace, he feels as though he is smiling from within. It is an emotion of pure joy in his core. When you are aware of the feeling you desire, it makes it easier to attract it. Hence, it is important to imagine yourself in the position you desire and allow yourself to experience all the emotions and sensations you expect when in that position. The Universe can only be as accurate as your instructions when providing what you desire.

Your need to be right feeds on your 'Don't Wants'

I remember watching a talk show as a teenager and one statement that has remained with me since then:

'Do you want to be right or do you want to be happy?'

I have asked myself that question on many occasions in my life and expect to do so many more times. By etching this question into your mental hard drive, you will be able to dissect several confusing situations with more ease than expected. In fact, this is one of the most important questions you may ever have to answer.

Humankind has an innate need to be right about everything. Put it down to ego, pride or the air we breathe, most have a tendency to say to others, 'I told you so', or, 'I knew that'. The need of keeping a jump ahead usually overshadows our wish to be happy. Unfortunately, often the things we insist on being right about are actually negative factors. For instance making statements such as:

\# Life is not a bed of roses.
\# Money is the root of all evil.
\# All men are bastards.
\# All women are manipulative.
\# If I am single then I am not loved.
\# Money does not come easy.
\# I am not good enough.
\# It's not easy to be rich.
\# Relationships are hard work.

Have you ever thought any of these disempowering thoughts, notions? I am sure there are many such judgements you have made about life that you aren't even aware of. I know I have. What later proves to be a self-fulfilling prophecy, where you subconsciously create circumstances in your life to be right about one or all the so-called 'facts'. I recall a few years ago in June, my neighbour and I were watching television when I turned to her and said, 'You know what, I haven't been sick all year and I always fall sick in winter.'

Lo and behold, within the next few days I had the flu. This is a classic example of how we attract exactly what we *don't* want into our lives. We are so attached to being right that we almost *will* these negative things to be true. The woman who believes that all men are jerks will continually attract the man who is wrong for her while she allows him to treat her in a way she does not like and in the end gets to be right about them all being jerks.

The man who believes all women are manipulative will inadvertently lay traps and create situations for the woman to appear like she was being manipulative. People often do exactly what we expect or fear them to do.

Similarly, some of us will subconsciously want to spend every earned cent just to be right about always being broke. Some will eat themselves silly to be right about how hard it is to lose weight. It is these negative, self-doubting beliefs that attract more of what we *don't* want. We will subconsciously attract the 'wrong' type of people and situations into our lives to help us act out our self-fulfilling prophecies, because the desire to be right is so much stronger than the desire to be happy. The Universe is not discerning, it will respond to our highest vibration energies and return more of the same to us.

The sooner you decide that it is alright to believe the opposite of what the masses do, and that is it alright to trust the Universe, and you choose to be happy rather than to be right, the sooner you *will* be happy.

Walk the talk

The Universe does not respond to our words or our thoughts, merely thinking positive is not enough. The Universe responds to how we are *vibrating*. Our vibrations are a direct result of how we are feeling.

Remember the convertible I coveted and then owned? Another thing I did apart from pasting pictures of it on my walls was I felt it was already mine. When I drove my old car, I felt as if I were already driving the convertible. I had the windows down to emulate the feeling of 'cool wind in my hair' and I smiled as if I were already in that car. These days in India, even when I am sometimes in a rickshaw, and I experience the same 'wind-in-my-hair' sensation, it conjures up the same joyous feeling of magic I had when I was actively manifesting my convertible and when I was really driving it 'top-down'. The feeling is the same...the vibrations are the same. Emulating something creates the same vibrations as actually doing it, that is the principle that astronauts in NASA use—simulators.

This is a simple principle called *'be, do, have'* or 'Being, Doing and then Having'.

Many of us say things like: *when I have that car, I will be happy*, or *when I lose weight, I will be able to learn dancing*, or *when I have a million or ten million dollars, I will be successful*. It is, in fact, all in reverse.

In this book, Plugging In & allowing is part of the 'being', taking action and moving forward is the 'doing' and the gratitude comes from the sense of already 'having'

To vibrate that positive feeling to manifest the thing or the situation we desire, we have to feel it in the present, as if we are already in it. When we are feeling it, we are 'being' who we need to be to 'do' the actions it would require so we can 'have' what we desire.

First steps

\# Be aware that we are *always* creating and manifesting. We don't stop.

\# Every time you even think of a 'don't want', you are creating that reality for yourself.

\# Trust that you are powerful and rethink, rephrase and focus on what you want. And *feel* as if you *already have it*. If you focus on wanting, you are reaffirming that you do not have it; the feeling is still of 'not having', so instead focus on the feeling that you already have what you want.

\# Smile, hold your head high at all times, take deep breaths and consciously see and feel what you want.

The more you focus on what you want, the more the Universe will respond to your positive, happy vibrations and give you more to be happy about. Merely *not* allowing yourself to think of what makes you happy is encouraging negative vibrations. So, not fantasising, not visualising or expecting happy and joyful situations in our lives is causing negative attraction. That is how powerful we are!

Use whatever tools or pleasure triggers you can think of to help you feel good (within reason, of course). Visualise yourself living the life you have always wanted. See yourself in situations that make you happy. Listen to music that makes you feel good and makes you smile. It works!

Indeed, you will risk looking like a looney-toon, smiling from ear to ear for no apparent reason, but you'll be the happy one and that will only manifest more happiness for you.

Thinking Pink Exercise for a New Beginning

List ten of your 'don't wants' and then opposite them list your 'wants' using positive language. Keep this list handy as you go on through the chapters.

2

Plugging In to Source

Faith consists in believing when it is beyond the power of reason to believe.

— *François-Marie Arouet (Voltaire)*

Everything is always perfect

Circumstances, even when you cannot see them, are exactly as they should be for you to manifest what you want. Even a traffic jam or your Internet being down could be a good thing in hindsight. We have all heard stories of people who were supposed to be on the Titanic's maiden voyage, but for various reasons they could not get to Southampton in time. At the time, most of them would not have looked at it as a good thing when they missed the boat; they were angry, upset and complaining about the 'inconvenience', some were deeply disappointed. But later, we can imagine they must have been overwhelmed by their good fortune in the grander scheme and perhaps may have even shed tears of gratitude.

Plugging In

No problem can be solved from the same consciousness that created it.

— *Albert Einstein*

The only difference between those of us who have what we want and live the lives we desire and those of us who don't, is how connected we are to the Universe. Some people have an abundance of everything they want from life—money, love, health, fitness, good relationships, meaningful friendships, happiness, joy, security, lots of fun and energy. They are the ones who are, as I like to put it, Plugged In. Establishing our own connection to the power of the Universe is very easy. We have the tools inside us to get connected right now, some prefer to call it prayer, meditation, centring, grounding or even just connecting. Call it what you will but it is establishing one's connection to the Source.

Think of yourself as a mobile phone and visualise the signal strength bars on your screen. Plugging In is re-establishing that connection to better your reception. Take a few moments and pray, but you could do it any way you like. Sit (on a chair or on the edge of your bed) with your feet planted on the ground, imagine energy flowing up from the earth to the soles of your feet and then through your body. Imagine it to look like sparks of electricity. Feel the power and connect.

Whenever I feel 'less of myself', or as if I am not as productive as I can be, or abundance is not flowing into my life, or I am not laughing and smiling as much, or my relationships seem stuck and difficult, it is an indication that I am losing that connection. It is like being in a 'bad service area' where calls drop out. That is my cue to find the space and quiet time, sit down and plug in. We cannot remain Plugged In at all times, but the aim is to notice when we have lost connection and take a few moments to reconnect.

I was brought up in a family who believed in the Bhagwad Gita. My father, as part of our daily ritual, got us to sit together as a family every evening to recite the 12th chapter, the Yoga of Devotion. Even our family dog, Snoopy, sat in the prayer room with us. I know it by heart now but even though I have read books that translate it, I would be lying if I said I fully understand it. However, I can recite it perfectly ad hoc, but despite that well-meaning ritual, I did not realise that my father was giving us the perfect opportunity to connect at least once a day. In hindsight, I feel almost like I had a phone without a sim card inserted in it. You just need to think about Plugging In and you are. It is as simple as that. Therefore, you could be practicing hours of rituals but if you do not think of it as you connecting to Source energy, you will remain disconnected.

My personal Plugging In started about a decade ago. And after practicing it, I learnt the secret—to have faith. To trust tacitly all the time, not only when it was convenient to trust, but *always*.

Going back to the metaphor of the signal bars on your phone, imagine that you are a telecommunication tower connected magnetically to the Universe. This is a little difficult to put into words but if you Plug In even slightly, then you know the Universe is everywhere around you. We can call it Source, Universe, God, Higher Self, Inner Self, Soul, whatever name you choose to call it, you are Plugged In *to* it.

Given that you agree that everything connects to everything else, that you are a part of a higher energy, this chapter is to help you enforce that connection with that energy, wherever you choose to believe it exists, up in the heavens, down in the earth or in yourself.

Take a few minutes every day or if you like several times a day to Plug In. How do you Plug In? This can be personal for many of us, but find a practice that helps you feel grounded and at the same time connected.

You can Plug In while listening to music, while driving, in silence, while dancing, I even do it in elevators or in the shower.

Plugging In through silence

Sit on a chair with your feet planted on the ground and both hands on their relative laps, relax your shoulders and close your eyes. Make sure that you are in an 'open-body' position. Your legs, feet and arms do not cross and your chest is open to receive. Feel the weight of your feet on the ground and of your hands on your lap. Inhale and exhale slowly, imagining your breath going all the way down to your stomach and then feel the weight of your feet on the ground even heavier. You can imagine there are roots coming out and down from your feet, which are growing deep down into the ground. If you are in a tall building on a high floor, I like to imagine these roots are running all the way down to ground zero. Then imagine the roots going into the ground, just like the roots of a huge old oak tree.

Simultaneously, imagine that your head can open to receive all the brightness and light energy from the skies and the Universe. To me, this looks like bright white sparks or lightning.

Accept all your thoughts, and let them go, do not ponder on any too long and breathe normally.

This is the perfect time for a prayer or an affirmation where you ask for connection. 'Please come and express yourself clearly through me', is the one I use when I am about to coach or write.

This is not egotistical or arrogant, in fact it is the opposite, it is where you give up your ego and need to be in control of everything.

To take it further, imagine yourself Plugged In...and wherever you go the imaginary long extension cord connected to you follows. The only time it loses its connection bar-signals is when you forget that you are indeed connected. So all you need to do is to think of being Plugged In and you are.

Decide on a trigger or a visual to help you to remember and get a sense of being Plugged In. I sometimes think of the roots below my feet as I walk and I also look up to the ceiling or sky to re-establish my contact. I even visualise the plug going into the socket. Have fun with this and come up with your own ways of getting a sense of feeling Plugged In.

The empowering belief here, and it is my invitation to take it on, is that *everything is perfect*, even the situations that do not seem so. Everything is as it should be and can be. Once you believe this all the time, you will see that your implicit faith is what gives your dreams the opportunity to manifest.

Plugging In through movement

Have you ever gone to the gym and, while exercising, experienced a sense of peace and being in the moment? Your phone is switched off and far away and the only thing you are aware of is your body? You are aware of your breathing, you can feel the pain and the stretch in your muscles and the specific ligaments that are being used. You are Plugged In through body. You cannot be aware of your body and your breath without being Plugged In.

Have you ever danced and swayed to music, feeling the rhythm in your feet and in your heart? Music is a great way to experience being present and being grounded.

Pick two songs you that make you feel like moving your body and listen to them again and again to become familiar with the beats, notice the lyrics, the pauses and the melodies so you can pre-empt them. Then find a quiet space where you can be alone and allow yourself to move to the music. Try different movements with your arms and feet. Smile and move to the music. Allow yourself to express your *self* through your movements. You don't have to be a professional dancer to do this alone. No one is watching you. Get into the music and lose yourself to the melody and the beats. Dance like nobody's watching!

You can even Plug In when you sleep

Sleep is another way to Plug In. Connect every night before you sleep, start a ritual, writing in *gratitude journal* is a great way to end your day and open your mind to positive thoughts. Say a prayer and ask for answers before you fall asleep. Imagine you are holding in your cupped left hand a bright yellow ball, and before falling asleep visualise all your heart's desires in that ball. And then imagine the ball dissolving into your palm and the yellow liquid spreading all through your hand, arm, and body. You would usually fall asleep before you can even get to that part.

Plug In when you shower

Change your relationship with time. If you are like me, then I am always rushing to get there on time even when I have nowhere to get to. It is an old habit I developed—as a child who had to be in school at seven in the morning and always wanting to snooze a few extra minutes, as a single mum who had to have tea, breakfast and lunch boxes ready, uniform ironed and be dressed up smartly to drive my daughter to school and reach the office on time, so showers were rushed and had to be compromised. It is only recently that I learnt to take my time in the shower. One of the biggest treats you can give your body, mind and self is to take an extra five minutes in the bathroom, have a long shower, enjoy the smells and the aromas, texture, pressure and temperature in the shower, followed by taking a few minutes to truly relish that luxurious cream on your skin. Why are you rushing? If you are always late, then allow extra time, again, you cannot be feeling your own body, aware of your pulse, breath and the texture of your skin and not be Plugged In.

Have you ever booked yourself in for a haircut, then sitting there you get impatient and cannot wait for it to be over? Stop and breathe and enjoy having your hair cut. People go to the gym for a workout or for Yoga, and they keep looking at the time, anxious for it to get over. Relish, enjoy and love your experiences, allow them to nurture and love you back.

We do not require constant social interaction. We do not always need to be with people. Have you ever enjoyed your own company? Have you ever tried to ask yourself for answers or do you always speed dial your closest friend, your partner, your mother or father even whenever you are faced with a choice or an option? I have my brother Sanjay to thank for this, he used to be on my speed dial list, and the habit prevented me from trying to feel or think for myself until his advice to me one such time was to Plug In and be at source. Nowadays, again out of an old habit, I still send him emails and instant messages asking for his advice but even before he can reply, I know that I just need to Plug In.

Practice being 'at source'

Sit in a café. Avoid using your phone to sms/bbm/ping/whatsapp/fb/browse, play Texas hold-em or Sudoku. Be open to your surrounding and the people around you. Notice the sights, the sounds and the taste that is around you and feel the appreciation for it all.

If you do not take the time to be with yourself, in your own space, you miss Plugging In to the Universe and connecting with your *self*. Moreover, in that you miss recognising all your 'angels' or people who will nourish and nurture your life and you theirs.

Only when you are being yourself, can you love someone or be with him or her truly. Honour your own wants, desires and dreams. Trust your own taste, judgements and choices before you can share yourself with anyone.

Once you are Plugged In you will experience the power of connectedness and coincidences will not seem isolated or unrelated any more.

Accept not knowing

I used to be the sort who needed to know everything. How everything would work, all the steps and strategies of a particular project, where everyone was and what everyone was saying, thinking or doing.

My biggest fear was that something bad would happen and it would hit me by surprise. I would not be expecting it, I would be the last to know and look stupid. Looking stupid and being unprepared was what I feared more than the occurrence of 'bad' events in my life. So to 'protect' myself from this 'not-knowing-ness', I would conjure up in my mind all the possible terrible things that could be going on 'behind-my-back' so when it all came out, I could say to everyone and especially to myself, 'I KNEW THIS WAS GOING TO HAPPEN'. My fear that the undesirable thing would happen and that I would be seen as unprepared or naïve was stronger than the fear of the actual event. So when I was offered a project, I would think negative thoughts like, 'Oh, this is not going to work out, I am sure they won't agree to the terms, you can never rely on these big companies', or when I met a perfectly nice man and he asked me out, I would 'warn' myself that it would not last or that he would show his 'true-colours', 'He must be seeing other women', 'He's pretending to have a good job, when actually he is living off borrowed funds', 'he's gay'.

I would talk about it to my friends, laying out all the things that would go wrong, so that when the project did get cancelled or shelved, or when things did not work out in the relationship, I got to appear prepared, like I knew it all along and I was not caught unaware.

I have worked with men and women who would plant seeds of doubt about the integrity of their spouses and suspect them of cheating on them saying, 'Do you think I am a fool', 'do you think I don't know what it going on behind my back'. This way of thinking is what leads the relationship to destruction. All for the desperate need to look like a 'know-it-all' in the end. Again here, you see how the need of 'being right' supersedes the desire to be happy.

This behaviour is, by the way, the easiest way to sabotage any relationship or venture. It becomes a self-fulfilling prophecy. Now we know that, our thoughts become our realities. What you think about, especially with feelings and passion, will manifest in your world. Therefore, I manifested all the 'bad' or negative things into my life, just so I could be 'right'. I did not like it when people around me said 'I told you so', 'we warned you', so I also had to expect the bad things to happen in 'preparation' so that I got to look all clever and prepared in the end.

That was back when I had not learnt to Plug In and trust yet; today my belief is so strong that I do not allow myself to dwell for a moment in thoughts of sadness, sickness, poverty or betrayal. I can filter it soon enough and replace that disempowering thought, vision, feeling with an empowering one.

The important thing to remember is to quickly change and replace your thoughts and feelings. A quick way to do this is by tapping on your pleasure list (more on pleasure lists in Chapter 5), which is a great tool to use to have easy 'on-tap' access to 'feel-good' activities to switch to, whenever we entertain doubt. Simply put, 'the need to know' is just worry and doubt, which you will stop entertaining in your world. Trusting implicitly means to leave no room for any doubts. Trust and doubt cannot exist in the same space. Through practice, positive reinforcement and the manifestation of your desires, you will realize that the only way to have what you want is to trust that you will have it and to expect it, without doubt.

Apart from creating these negative outcomes in my life through my need to 'know' all the possible 'bad' things that could happen, I took this a step further. I would not go with a possibly 'good' idea because I did not know how it was going to work out. I was too afraid of what I did not know, the *hows*, the next step and the future.

Worrying about how things would fall into place, I held myself back from stepping toward positivity to make things happen in my life.

My need to know not only attracted negative circumstances into my life, it prevented positive things from coming into my life, too. Talk about a double whammy! The big lesson for me was to accept *not knowing*. It is 'OK' to not know. Even if undesirable things were going to happen, it is 'OK' to be caught by surprise. We are all strong enough to face and overcome them if we have to. Now my faith is so strong that I can almost remove myself from an undesirable circumstance, look at it from a higher place and trust that 'this too shall pass'. And that everything does happen for my highest good, even if I cannot see it at the time and even if it hurts while I have to go through the transition. My mum brought us up with that adage, 'this too shall pass', but it took me many years to imbibe and believe it.

My younger brother was working on my website and he being the expert that he is, designed some 'html', 'flash' thing that I could not comprehend. My old need resurfaced, to need to know how and why he designed it the way he did, for what purpose and what it would do. Being more Plugged In than me often, he humoured me by explaining all the technical details using words and acronyms I had never heard before and he spoke at about a thousand words per minute. Getting his point, I said, 'Ok, Vishaal, I trust you, I don't need to know how, I just need to trust you.'

I learnt that it was also 'OK' to not know why or how all the good stuff was going to come into my life, and in spite of the not-knowingness, be able to trust the Universe implicitly and know that the outcome was going to be desirable. When we are willing to say, 'Universe, I cannot figure this out, so I am going to trust U (I deliberately used 'U' to symbolise Universe) to unravel the path before me,' then you can be comfortable in spite of not knowing. Trusting implicitly often requires not knowing how exactly things are going to fall into place. Not knowing where the much needed money or resource is going to come from, not knowing when it will come. Not knowing how a situation that seems so bleak and hopeless is going to work itself out for the highest good of all concerned. Not knowing how you are going to accomplish all that you have set out to do. Not knowing how anything is going to work out, but knowing in your heart that it will.

The Universe is never late, but generally, it is not early either. Why not early? To test our implicit trust, perhaps. If everything we asked for came to us immediately, we would never grow and develop. Timing and trust work side by side. As we develop patience, we feel completely satisfied. Faith is the antidote for this doubt and fear, so cultivate the belief that everything is in order, everything is perfect and the Universe is conspiring for your highest good—even when it doesn't look or sound like it.

In my experience though, this is a classic egg and chicken scenario. Which comes first, the belief or the trust? Practice the principles and look for validation and you will be converted. However, of course, you have to be willing to believe first. Reading books on the Law of Attraction certainly opens up your world to new possibilities but results only come from believing and practicing. *Ask, Believe and Receive*. And having a partner hold your hand while you do this is priceless. Remember, thinking positive is not enough; we have to FEEL positive vibes in order to attract more of what we want and less of what we do not.

Perhaps because I have manifested repeatedly, I trust the Universe implicitly. Things, circumstances are exactly as they should be in order for you to realise and manifest what you want. Even when you cannot for the life of you see it. Imagine that once you have asked and you have declared that you are going to have a certain something, the universe arranges all its pieces—like a 1000 piece jigsaw puzzle box being thrown in the air and having to all fall into place to create this picture that you have conjured up in your mind. Imagine that this is occurring in slow motion, some pieces have to move up in order for others to move down. If you were to take a snap shot of this process in motion, it would look chaotic...you would not be able to see the finished picture at all. This is a part of the Jigsaw Puzzle Visualisation Exercise, which will be clearly explained in Chapter 3.

This is where unspoken trust comes in. Even the most inconvenient occurrences, like the global economic crisis are necessary for the pieces to fall into the perfect place that is for your highest good.

Anyone who has ever been house or used-car hunting would surely be able to connect with the Jigsaw Puzzle Visualisation Exercise. You see three different ones and then you like one and by the time you go to make your offer, somehow it does not work out because of some detail, you may be disappointed, then you feel like you have to start from scratch again. And then through a series of events you finally seal the deal on one flat or car and you are incredibly happy that all the others did not work out because of the timing and synchronicity that needed to take place in order for you to find this one. I have experienced this so many times that now when something does not go in accordance with the plan, I don't get disappointed anymore, I actually get excited about what better experience is making its way to me.

Safety nets are for amateurs

Having safety nets in place is a sure way to ensure you do not succeed at manifesting. People want safety nets to protect themselves from falling, however they are only affirming that you will fall and you do not trust the process. It requires fearlessness and implicit faith to manifest, as soon as you have a glimmer of doubt, no matter how much you do, feel, vibrate, and affirm, you are showing the Universe that you do not really believe, you are just 'trying' out the concept. An iota of doubt is enough to prevent the manifesting. When you want to achieve big things in life, you have to take a leap of faith. I recall someone saying to me that they have often seen me standing on a tiny ledge and they have gasped, scared for me, and they either turned away or closed their eyes because they could not help and neither could they look for they were so sure that this time I was going to fall off. However, by the time they came back, they saw me flying again on the back of an angel to greater heights than ever imagined.

People often need to have safety nets in place before they try something they consider dangerous, whether it is an entrepreneurial project or even a relationship prospect. They would have a back-up option for each endeavour: I am calling it endeavour because it is a trial—there is not faith that it will work out and soar. With love, they would hedge their bets, making sure that there was someone else to fall back on if this one did not work out, some would even keep both options believing that they are the only one. They would always hold back and prevent themselves from being vulnerable for the fear of getting hurt. The danger of this is that you are revealing an underlying desire just to 'try'. Often this comes from what you think people expect of you and not what you truly desire for yourself. You want to be able to say to everyone that at least you tried. This behaviour is painful and it takes up so much time and energy, often trying to do something and doing it requires the same amount of work, the only difference is in your resilience when the going becomes a little slow and your journey reaches a plateau. Having a safety net in place will allow you to give up just before the time you would have succeeded. People have often asked me how I soar higher every time they have seen me almost fall, and I think the only answer is that I have implicit faith in the Universe. I am on the journey and path that is mine. Despite the odds in the eyes of onlookers, I keep at it, working at it, learning and practicing all the time patiently, because there is no safety net and I know that falling is not an option.

Without a doubt
When you put the kettle on, you know that in a few minutes the water is going to boil, you do not need to sit and stare at it while also looking at the time wondering when it will reach boiling point. It is a given.

Think of someone in your personal or professional life that you truly can rely on, a person that you do not doubt at all. Have you ever tried calling this person or sending a text message to them and they did not pick up or reply? You are calm and relaxed and you know that they are probably busy with something important, or perhaps in the shower, and you have no doubt that as soon as they see your missed call or message on their phone, they will return your call. And you go about your time in ease, with absolutely no attachment to the attempt you made to call them. Compare this same scenario to when you call someone that you are unsure of, and the same thing happens, he or she does not pick up your call or reply your message immediately, this is a man or woman you are interested in, or someone you are doing business with and you are unsure about this person. You go into irritation and anxiety, you do not trust this person, you convolute stories in your head that they do not like you, or they are not interested in the deal, or they are avoiding you or that he or she is playing games with you. You may even check your phone to make sure it is working. You get impatient. All this is because you do not trust them. In order to manifest, you have to trust the Universe *implicitly* as you do your trusted friend, be calm and get on with your day in ease and comfort knowing without a doubt that *IT* will deliver.

Very soon you will not be surprised when you make things happen anymore, you will instead be grateful and sometimes even awed but not surprised. I have been able to 'make' a rainbow appear when I have wanted to. The car I wanted became mine to own. It is fun. The Law works. I write in my gratitude journal every night. First I would struggle to think of things to be grateful for, then I started going through my days noticing all the things I am grateful for, making mental notes to write them down at night in my journal, then I started writing names of the people who touched my life that day and since then, everyday is more beautiful than the last. When I was in the process of writing this book and I started the chapter on Gratitude, I realised that it would be awesome if people had a special sacred space to write in every single night and only in gratitude. This led to the creation of *Thankfulness, Appreciation Gratitude—My Journal* that was my first publication and turned me from Life Coach to Author in 2011. Nowadays, I present a copy to all my clients and encourage them to instill the habit of writing just a few lines every night in gratitude. It changed my life and from all the feedback and loving testimonials I have received from people who have been diligently writing in the journal, I know that it has changed many people's lives too.

If you were familiar with Mumbai as a city, you would know that to find an apartment to rent within a budget with a gym would be impossible. When I was looking for a place, the very night before I saw this particular one that I did make my home, while I practiced my nightly Plugging In, a passing thought came to my mind to 'add to' my apartment wish-list desire, a small gym with at least a treadmill.

I had been looking for a place for two weeks so obviously my thoughts were around finding the right place. Even as I thought it, I remember saying to myself, 'Malti, this is Mumbai and you have a budget.' Still I said it and visualised it before dozing off. The next day, the broker showed me this place and I liked it and was already beginning to negotiate rent on the way out but then as I stepped out of the lift, I saw a door slightly ajar and someone walking on a treadmill.

I started practicing the Sutra Statements in Deepak Chopra's *Synchrodestiny*.

Imagine that the whole universe is a vast ocean of consciousness, and your intentions shoot out from within your heart and ripple across the vast ocean of consciousness.

I have a 'parking, God' moment every time I go anywhere. I never think about parking, and I get a spot that is most convenient without having to look for one. But every time someone else is in the car with me and merely raises the question 'Where are you going to park?' and if I start doubting it, I don't get parking. Doubt is not an active thing we do, the mere absence of trust, when we start to question, is doubt. Trust the Universe Implicitly. If you walk away with nothing else today, but to say this and believe in 'I trust the Universe Implicitly', I assure you, your life will change.

People often behave exactly how we expect them to behave with us. If we trust, they are trustworthy. If we doubt, they will let us down, because that is all we expect from them. Watch this one with your kids, if you expect them to do well in an exam, they often will. It is true of expecting them to fail miserably, too.

Circumstances often turn out the way we expect them to. My definition of *'Confidence'* is – *always expecting a positive outcome*. When you walk into a situation, be it personal or professional, when you expect things to go well, you are confident and more often than not, that confidence you exude is what attracts the positive result. Our surroundings are a direct and proportional reflection of our own state of being, which leads me to an experiential learning exercise I participated in—I had to climb up a ten-metre telephone pole, the circumference of the actual pole was just a little wider than my feet, say 30cm. Sure, I was fully harnessed and it was in a perfectly 'safe' environment, in fact there was an actual safety-net. But when I got up there and had to stabilise before jumping off, I felt that my world was shaking. The pole was shaking and I was petrified. Later, I realised that it was my own fear that caused me to tremble and shake, which in turn caused the pole to shake. We effect our surroundings in a much bigger way than we can imagine. So, the next time you find yourself in a hostile situation, in an uncomfortable place, not trusting anyone or anything, do a quick check to see where all the vibrations are truly coming from.

Questions on Plugging In:

How to be more confident?

Expect only positive outcomes—all the time. No such thing as 'more' confident, you are confident or you are not! You expect positive results or you expect negative results.

Shall I trust and have faith or should I fear and doubt?

Trusting opens doors. Fear paralyses you. FEAR is just False Evidence Appearing Real. Asking the Universe or your angels for help is one of the most powerful spiritual practices.

We are asking God or asking our higher self to come up with answers and solutions. Most of us do not realise or trust this power that we have to ask, believe and receive. It all begins with trust and being willing to believe against all odds and against what other people may think or how they may judge us for having this much faith. Like they say, 'Would you rather be stupid or happy?' As in, you may look silly for having this faith and practicing it, however, wouldn't you rather be happy?

Thinking Pink Exercise to Plugging In

When you wake up in the morning, set your feet on the ground and say a prayer to the Universe, 'If today is my last day, let it be my best,' and smile.

Before you go to bed, ask to sleep in peace, dream for what you need to learn and wake up in joy.

Anytime you are not feeling good during the day, take it as an invitation to Plug In and do it in any short ritual you can. Take a few deep breaths, close your eyes, relax your mind, be 'OK' with all your thoughts and feelings and add a quick visualisation of being Plugged In using whatever imagery you prefer. You can use *roots going into the ground from your feet, energy sparks coming into your head and going up into the sky, a plug going into a socket*, or *signal bars on a telephone going to full strength*. As long as you can feel it, you are Plugged In.

Write it down on a piece of paper 'I trust the Universe IMPLICITLY, ALL the time'. Stick this on a wall in your room where you will see it every day.

3
Making it Public

You get whatever accomplishment you are willing to declare.
— *Georgia O'Keefe*

Make the decision
To achieve your desire, you must first make a conscious 'Decision'. With making a decision starts the entire process of getting what you want and the instant you decide, the wheels are set in motion. For instance, I decided to consult a healer about an ailment. I was suffering from a dull ache that started at the right side of my throat and travelled, increasing in intensity all the way through my right hip, down to my foot. Driving a vehicle in itself was an ordeal as stepping on the accelerator only sent excruciating pain shooting up my leg. I tried visiting a chiropractor but to no avail. However, when I paid for my phone consultation with the healer, I sealed my decision and knew I was already healing. True enough, after he administered his remedy the pain vanished and both my fitness instructor and chiropractor were amazed. The strange thing is I started to feel relief before my consultation with him began. I felt it the moment I decided to have faith in him.

No one can *see* you deciding, but they will almost always see the results of your decisions. When you have the confidence to declare these decisions, you breathe power into them. Think of it as inflating a balloon with helium and imagine it growing bigger as you pump more 'power' (helium) into it. The conviction you demonstrate by declaring your decision is the energy that fuels your desires. Once the objective succeeds in your mind, it is only a matter of time before the goal manifests for all to see. Imagine that *deciding* is just like turning on a switch. We don't need to have an understanding of how electrons flow and we do not need to demystify electricity. All we need to know is the light will come on when we flick the switch.

At the other end of the spectrum is 'Indecision', which causes splintering. How often have you heard a person saying, 'I don't know what to do?' And how often have you said, 'What should I do?' Think about some of the indecisive feelings you have experienced.

- *Love them / Leave them*
- *Quit / Stay*
- *Do it / Don't do it*
- *Go bankrupt / Don't go*
- *Go to work / Watch TV*
- *Move / Stay*
- *Buy it / Don't buy it*
- *Say it / Don't say it*
- *Tell them / Don't tell them*
- *Marry / Wait*

Can you identify the real culprit here? It is lack of confidence. Decision makers are not afraid of making mistakes. They know that if they make a 'wrong decision', they will learn from it and move on. They weigh the potential results and not only brace themselves for the potential outcomes but are willing to accept the consequences. They have already decided what the potential benefits of their decision are and they are ready to face and accept the way the situation unravels based on the decision they made. Indecision however, likens to hesitating at the traffic signal when it is amber and about to turn red. When we hesitate for too long, we put ourselves in a vulnerable position. Speed through or stop, evaluate the risks, mentally calculate the distance you have to go versus the oncoming traffic, choose one and live with the results.

We need to trust that once we decide and ask for what we want, it is already ours in the spiritual realm. It may take some time to manifest itself in the physical realm for all to see it, but start believing that it is already yours and feel the joy of already having it. Be grateful and thank the Universe since it is making its way to you. Picture yourself asking someone to throw you a ball and as you stand there, you prepare your hands and body expecting to catch it. In fact, I have started writing what I am *going* to be thankful for based on my decisions, in my *TAG (Thankfulness, Appreciation, Gratitude)* journal the next day, before I have seen it happen.

To be able to decide soundly, you have to understand the situation and the context compared to what matters most to you and your highest objectives. Being clear on your values and your desires will guide you.

How you decide to respond to a situation rather than reacting impulsively is strongly determined by your values and your desires. Aristotle's quote below refers to anger, but you can apply it to almost any reaction you may have.

Anybody can become angry – that is easy, but to be angry with the right person and to the right degree and at the right time and for the right purpose, and in the right way—that is not within everybody's power and is not easy.

Deciding your finance

Personal finance is one of the major concerns individuals worry about daily, especially in this economic climate. Knowing whether you *can* afford a particular thing or not is of no great significance. Rather, whether you *want* to or not, *is* the only real consideration. All the money in the world is available to you when the decision is firm. Once you decide you will find the money...every time. Know you *can* afford anything for the Universe is abundant and is here to support your desires.

The Universe does not understand money. Money was one of humankind's greatest inventions to barter for goods and services. The Universe understands 'Universal Abundance' as energy. So when making your declaration, make sure you are channeling the money towards your higher good and the higher good of all concerned. In other words, when you want something that costs money, focus on the 'thing' or the experience you want to have. When you spend that money, foresee it in a way it is enriching your life. Also, think of it as a transaction benefiting other people. Even when you buy a bunch of flowers, acknowledge to yourself that the shopkeeper, his family, the orchard and the entire town where the flowers grow will in some way receive a portion of that 'money' and benefit. Thus, you serve as an instrument for the energy of universal abundance to flow through.

Recently a close friend of the family, Martin, shared an example of Universal Abundance with me. He loved his rickety old car, which took him from point A to B on 'no-petrol'. He raved about how he had forgotten to top-up fuel before getting on the highway and his gauge was pointing at 'E' for empty and therefore flashing red, but after willing the car on to 'make it' and thrusting his desires in to the Universe to manifest, he managed to get home. At the end of his trip, he calculated that he had driven over 800 kilometres on $50 of petrol while most other cars would only travel for 500 kilometres for the same amount. This is a great example of Universal Abundance. It would not surprise you to know that in his head the 'E' for Empty translated to 'E' for Enough to him. Your needs fulfil and you can do what you want to do, without actually receiving money in a conventional sense. I continuously feel supported in my life in this way. In the past, there were moments when I did not know where my next rent cheque would come from and then, as if by magic, it was provided. Sometimes it was an unexpected tax-refund, a windfall, or a new client paying me in advance. The point is, the Universe provided.

Some may scoff at the idea and think it is absurd. Their old and limiting way of thinking will say, 'You cannot decide to do something if you do not have the necessary resources!' The truth is that way of thinking will only keep them where they are always waiting. Albert Einstein aptly defined 'insanity' as *doing the same thing over and over again and expecting different results*. They will always be able to find reasons and justify why they do not have what they say they want. Ask yourself, would you rather have a life of reasons or results? Time and money are just excuses. We have all experienced that moment in our lives when we desperately wanted to do something or go somewhere and once we decided to go ahead no matter what, like divine intervention, both the money and the time were taken care of. When you catch yourself saying, 'I would like to do or have this but I can't because...' Whatever follows 'because' is the excuse. Excuses may cause a detour in your life, but you should never allow them to prevent you from making important decisions.

We have all made decisions in advance about life...like how we would react when faced with certain situations. Some of these 'advanced decisions' are great at keeping us on track but others can be both limiting and destructive. Several years ago, I decided I would build a relationship on honesty and hold out for someone who possessed all the qualities I felt were important in a partner. This was a great way for me to weed out individuals who did not live up to my 'wish list' and attract the ones who could accept my truths and had the qualities that I desired. Deciding like that in advance can help prevent unnecessary heartache in the end. Most of us also decide never to break the law; having pre-decided this makes it so much easier to choose when faced with options. Often, there is the legal way or the 'under-the-table' way; someone who has decided to stay on the right side of the law would hear the niggling voice at the back of their minds when about to download pirated movies from the Internet, they would not make that illegal U-turn on a highway, and they definitely would not walk out of a restaurant without paying, *on purpose*. We decide in advance. When we face the appropriate situations, we already know what we will do. It is important to be aware of the decisions we make in advance and if they are empowering and encourage progress, change and growth, if they help keep us aligned to our values, they are usually good ones to stick to. However, if they are limiting and negative, perhaps it is time to re-evaluate them.

An example of a limiting, disempowering 'advanced decision' would be to say or feel, 'I am shy.' When we have already decided we are shy, we turn away from opportunities in life that invite us to step up. We turn down the invitation to be fearless and get onstage to dance, show off a talent, write a book, respond to an advertisement or walk up to that gorgeous girl or guy to ask for their number. The decision 'I am shy' is a great excuse to hold us back. A good way to test your decision-making powers is to say to yourself that you are confident and that 'being shy' was a statement you made about yourself when you were younger and you behaved shyly. It does not mean that you *ARE* still a shy person. Making limiting decisions like that can hold you back from experiencing some of life's most enriching moments. So, look at every new opportunity as a time to make a new decision about yourself.

The power of declaration
How often have you...

\# felt something, but held back and didn't say it to anyone?

\# landed the job, but you have not started yet, so you keep it to yourself?

\# met the girl of your dreams, and things are going well, but you don't know how long it will last. So you remain evasive when friends and family ask you about your life?

\# started this amazing diet and fitness regime, but you are not sure if you will lose the weight?

\# quit smoking, but you are not sure if you will last?

\# been pregnant, but scared you may miscarry?

\# healed of the disease, but afraid it may come back?

\# started a business and it is going well, but you are scared you may fall?

\# had your lawyers say that they are confident you will win the case, but you don't tell a soul, in case it goes wayward?

The reason we do not declare is that we *doubt* and therefore are afraid of failing in front of others. However, when you start believing in yourself and in the Universe then you will be able to declare confidently your intentions knowing in your gut that you *will* succeed. For many cultures, this can be ingrained in your genetic make-up and we do not talk about possible good things for fear we may 'jinx' it. Practice and, if you are superstitious, touch wood if you have to, but practice saying the good things.

I was once at a workshop on *Intentions* and to show the power of intention and declaration, the speaker, my brother Sanjay told the group of attendees that he was going to break a ceramic tile using a light bulb. I had my doubts, but he declared, 'With clear intention, you get clear results. There is POWER when you are clear on what you want.'

We watched as he repeatedly dropped the light bulb on the ceramic tile, which was on the floor. It took three tries, and each time the bulb did not shatter, and finally when for the third time he dropped the light bulb, *the tile* split into four pieces, not the glass light bulb! We were all amazed and had to pick up those pieces to check whether it was in fact ceramic.

There is a scientific explanation to this, as explained by David Willey, from the Physics Department of The University of Pittsburgh, 'I think that the tile broke, rather than the light bulb, because of their shapes. The light bulb is almost spherical in shape, more important, the curve is symmetrical about an axis through the top and bottom of the bulb. This is an extremely strong shape. Try squeezing an egg when holding it between your thumb and index finger (at the tip and bottom of the longitude oval shape)—you will not be able to break it. Turn it sideways so the arch is not symmetrical, now it is easily broken.

'Both the tile and the glass of the light bulb are strong in compression, but weak in tension. When the bulb drops on the tile the bulb does not break because only compressive forces act on it, the tile however has its top surface compressed, but the bottom is put in tension, hence it breaks'.

Despite the scientific explanation, as Sanjay puts it, the science is 10 per cent and the intent is the balance 90 per cent. Sanjay says that those who do not believe it is possible, and even though they have the technique right, will still go through a few cartons of light bulbs before breaking a tile.

After declaring your desired result, picture it in your mind's eye. This is like fantasising, like how men do about Paris Hilton or women about Brad Pitt. For it to be real, it first has to be a thought. When your mind has already 'seen' the desired picture, image or movie, it can send out the vibration energy needed into the spiritual realm to start the alchemy of it to manifest in the physical world. As Napolean Hill, author of the age-old book on manifesting wealth, *Think and Grow Rich* wrote, *Whatever your mind can conceive and believe it can achieve*. (Quoted here with consent from The Napolean Hill Foundation. www.naphill.org)

Once you have done this, the only other thing to do is to trust and to allow.

I decided I wanted to lose some weight, so I declared in February 2008 to all my friends that I was going to be a particular weight by July 10, 2008. I shopped for clothes of a smaller size and not my current measurements. Declaring that I would fit into those clothes kept me committed to making it happen by sticking to my eating and fitness plan. When the time came, the clothes fit perfectly! We declared that we would have this book published by June 2012 and here it is. I thought of myself at book-signing engagements internationally and that, too, came to be.

Have you ever worked on a large jigsaw puzzle to put together a beautiful image? The finished picture is usually on the box and even though the packaging boasts one thousand pieces, to the ardent puzzle fan it seems easy enough to put together. To illustrate the workings of the Universe, try the following exercise. Read it first and then close your eyes, Plug In and practice it.

Jigsaw Puzzle Visualisation Exercise
With your eyes closed, imagine a blank screen as wide as you can. In the middle of this screen, see yourself. Imagine what you are wearing, your desired body shape and conjure an image that would clearly depict you are living that desired life. Feel the joy and gratitude and physically change your posture to open your chest and look upwards, inhale and smile right now.

In your image, see yourself smiling and looking ecstatically happy. Now slowly add the people you want. Your loved ones, and if you are not in a romantic relationship and want to be in one, then see yourself in an embrace with someone. See the two of you holding each other and yourself beaming with love and joy. Do not give this person a definite face. The vision is about *your* desires, so the focus is on *you* and *your* face. If there are any material desires you want to manifest, add them to the same image. You will have to get creative here, imagine you are a movie director and you can place props and people wherever you like.

So if it is a home, perhaps imagine you are in it or standing outside; if it is a car, then see yourself standing next to it with its key in hand; if it is holidays then see yourself there. You are the director and the choreographer and this is the edited version of the video, so only see the good scenes. Once you have a few of your strongest current desires in the image, feel the joy some more. Add some sound and effects. Imagine music and the words you will be hearing people say to you when you have indeed manifested this vision, the 'Congratulations' and 'He did it', 'She did it', and everything! Smile some more and beam with joy. Now increase the intensity of this image.

You can even put your hand out and imagine you are turning up the volume, brightness and colours; imagine the image and sounds getting louder, brighter and more vibrant in colours. You can even become aware of the smells. Once you can see and experience it clearly, freeze the image. Then try to see this perfect picture on the box of a one-thousand-piece jigsaw puzzle. Picture yourself buying this 'Ravensburger' puzzle and taking it home. When you open the box, you find all these small pieces, each one containing a fragment of your picture. Envisage that once you have declared that you are going to have a certain something, the Universe needs to arrange all its pieces—so now imagine these tiny colourful pieces being thrown up in the air and if you can, close your eyes and imagine each part falling down in slow motion.

As you visualise this scenario occurring in a gravity-free slow-motion fall, you will see that some pieces have to move up for others to move down. If you were to take a snapshot of this in motion, it would look chaotic and you would not be able to see the finished picture at all. Trusting the Universe implicitly means to trust the pieces will all fall into place eventually to form your beautiful picture. This is when you know that every detour or hangup along the way is necessary.

When I just moved to India in 2010, I went on a mission to make life coaching a household term in India and I did everything I could to get my name and our work out. I met with presidents and leaders of networking groups, spoke to countless editors and journalists of local magazines and newspapers, I wrote a lot and I networked a lot. I must have given out at least 1000 of my cards in my first two months.

The old and established women's group 'Indus' invited me to present to the group on 'Plugging In to The Universe' on Tuesday, November 16, 2010. This date was set back in August and at that point I did not know where I would be on November 16. I declared and I committed to being in Mumbai for this wonderful privilege and the invitation was sent out to all the members, by post, in print.

On impulse, I decided to spend the Hindu new year, Diwali (November 5, 2010) in London, so off I went, scheduled to return to work and this talk way before time. Unfortunately, I was in a car accident in London and injured my coccyx (tailbone). The injury kept me in London a few extra days, I got on a flight on the night of the 15th, arrived in Mumbai early 16th, and presented for over an hour passionately and completely from the heart to this wonderful group of responsive women. I was standing up throughout the entire presentation and the Questions and Answers part, though, because I could not sit down. Then after that, I lost my voice on that day itself, I had no voice, severe laryngitis.

It was painful and horrible to have no voice. I got it back about 6 days later and I went writing in my gratitude journal immediately as I don't think I have ever been grateful for my voice, sometimes it takes losing something (hopefully just for a little while) to realise how thankful we are that we have it. Interesting that I lost my voice only after I finished the presentation and that I made it back to Mumbai in time and in one piece after the injury.

I was committed and I declared that I would be there, friends around me could not believe how I was going to do it, with my injury, but now we also know that I was holding-off, 'postponing' a severe sore-throat too, for after the presentation. When you want to do something, and you decide that you will, *you will*. Since I learnt how powerful the power of declaration was, I started to achieve everything that I dared to declare.

When I joined the social networking site, Facebook and created a Facebook Page, I declared that I would have 1000 'Likes' in 3 months. And I did it on the date that I had declared it for. This was before the time of receiving social media updates on mobile phones, so I remember being out at dinner and my daughter who was home and online at the time, sent me a text message to tell me that I had done it. This happened about 15 minutes before the end of the day. When you declare and announce it to people in your community—and in this case, I spread the word on Facebook and on all my other social media sites—you give it power and it attracts the support of that community.

I had also already prepared a graphic badge that said 1000 fans (fans, because earlier it was fans and now they are called 'Likes') that I knew I would publish on the fan page way before I achieved that coveted figure. This was my way of showing myself that I believed, without a doubt, it was going to 'happen'. 'Once you decide to take the first step towards your success, the Universe magically rearranges everything to make it all start happening for you. Your journey will have already begun.'

Publishing your wish-list is all about 'DECLARATION', it is like shouting it from the roof tops and declaring it to the world—the first step. Great revolutions have happened across the globe through the power of declaration. Mahatma Gandhi declared 'India will be free' and with that he inspired movements for civil rights and freedom in India and across the world and this made sure the declaration became a reality. Declaration becomes infectious, pieces fall in place and resources start pouring in.

What stops us from making declarations, then? Fear that we will not live up to them. If you have even been in a car accident or a near-accident, you will be familiar with the instant physiological changes that happen in your body when you experience fear, fear of pain and fear of death.

Fear of pain

The dentist's chair is a big trigger of fear for me. In fact, I have this fear of needles. I used to faint at the sight of them. I do not do that anymore, thanks to a Neuro Linguistic Programming (NLP) process, but I do feel the physiological changes happening in my body as soon as confronted with just the mere thought of needles. However, I am able to stop myself from fainting by catching it in time. What I feel is no different from the expression 'blood running cold'. I feel a physical pain just under my ribs, above the stomach. My mouth starts to salivate, my head gets heavy, my vision blurred. Anyone who has experienced a 'vaso-vagal' or fainted before will know what I am describing. If you have not then the closest thing I can ask you to imagine is the feeling you have when you are about to do something you deem dangerous and scary. Similar to the sensation you feel when you are about to dive down when sitting at the peak of a roller coaster.

Well, this is how I feel when I am about to take a needle. In addition, this fear of needles is escalated 100 decibels when that needle happens to be with a Dentist so you can imagine my plight when I am lying in a dentist's chair. My George Clooney look-a-like dentist was also gentle and kind, so he numbed the gums first with a local ointment before attempting to inject the local anaesthesia. He talked to me about my life coaching to distract me, then told me to close my eyes and I knew he was about to start. My body went into fear, absolute fear. I waited to feel the pain which, by the way, never came. I did not feel the injection at all. Speak to a mother who is about to go into labour and she would be fearful. Again, there, when I had my daughter, I was lucky that I anticipated a lot of pain, but did not experience any.

Then there was the time I was at a workshop where we were all going to walk on burning coals.

The trainer, Anthony Robbins raised the energy in the room and got us all chanting fearlessly before it was our turn to walk on the red burning coals. Again, the fear of pain was huge, but when I started walking, I felt nothing.

There is a scientific explanation to how this can be done, just as there was a scientific explanation to breaking the ceramic tile with a glass light-bulb. David Willey co-produced a video on the Physics of Fire-Walking, when he had joined the

University of Pittsburgh in 1975, and he believes 'that when one walks on fire, on each step the foot absorbs relatively little heat from the embers that are cooled, because coal is a poor conductor of heat, and do not have much internal energy to transmit as heat. Also, the layer of cooled charcoal between the foot and the rest of the hot embers insulates our feet from the coals.'

So what I understood from the physics side of it is that because our feet are made up of lots of water, which has an exceptionally high specific heat capacity while coals have a low SHC, our foot's temperature will change less than the coal's. Water has a high thermal conductivity and our excessive blood flow in our feet carries the heat away, spreading it.

When the coal cools down, it stops burning, and new heat is not generated, and with the person walking quite quickly, not much time is spent on the burning coal. Haven't you touched a hot pot on the stove for a second without burning yourself, whereas if you were to have kept holding it, it would have become unbearable? Similar principle, but here we are dealing with your feet (tougher than your hands) and coal (not as good a conductor of heat as your stainless steel pot).

Although it can be explained in physics, this does not discount the fear that I felt when I was about to walk barefooted on a dark night outside the Sydney Entertainment Centre, only illuminated by these burning coals, my fear was of pain and nothing else, the feeling of fear was acutely uncomfortable, the pain never came. The polar opposite of pain is pleasure. Most of us have two major motivators in life—to have more pleasure and get away from pain.

What would you be willing to declare if you knew that the expected or impending pain would not be as bad as we fear it will be? Like my experience at the dentist? How many people pass up on what could have been the most beautiful loving experiences because of the fear of getting hurt?

The lack of pleasurable things in our life is also pain on some level.

Like not being able to sleep on a bed can be painful to some, not being with the one you love can be painful, so on and so forth...

Therefore, my invitation to you is this:

Know that nothing is too painful. Know that you are strong enough to take most pain. Spend more time pursuing pleasure and less time being afraid of pain. *Declare your desires with no fear.*

To Desire is different from To Yearn

There is nothing wrong or greedy about having desires, you have to desire in order to manifest. Just notice, though, the difference between desire and yearning.

Have you heard people saying, 'I have prayed and prayed for this to happen, why it hasn't happened for me?' The fact is that they yearned. Yearning is painful, because it holds in it the belief that you will *never* have the thing you want because you do not deserve it.

What is the body doing when you are yearning? Have you ever experienced or seen someone praying with their eyes tightly shut and their hands clasped so tight that the blood flow stops? When breathing becomes constricted and your shoulders close in, it looks like excruciating pain and desperation. Think of the words in a yearning prayed, 'Please... Please... Please...' as if you are begging. This is clearly the prayer and thought that you do not deserve what you are asking for and your body closes to receiving anything.

What about when you barter with God, 'Please, please, give me this and I will devote my life to you forever.' Again, you do not feel that you deserve enough of your desires and you feel you have to pay for them in some expensive way.

Your emotion is of desperation and sadness and you are doing this so powerfully that the vibrations are emanating from you on the highest frequencies.

Can you see how this goes against everything we know about manifesting and being open to receiving your desires?

Desire is soft and trusting, it has the faith that you deserve what you are asking for and your body is relaxed and open, your eyes, if shut, are softly closed and you are ready to see and accept the signs and inspiration that want to come to you.

In order to manifest you have to *allow* and in order to allow you have to give up the *how* and the *when*, trust that what you desire is magnetised towards you.

If you have some firm beliefs like you do not deserve what you desire, then you have to check in with who you are being in the world and the ecology of your desires. Will the attainment of your desires help many others achieve their desires, too? Will it give you the stage to give more to the world and create a bigger community of people whose lives you can contribute to? Will it reaffirm your belief in your powers and then help you to desire more and more? Do you deserve what you desire? Are your actions and thoughts in alignment with what you feel will be for the higher good of everyone concerned?

If you answered 'NO' to any of these questions, then perhaps what you need to do first is to identify all that you need to rewrite, do and be in order to become more deserving. The Universe does not discern, you will get what you desire but you are discerning and if you feel that you are undeserving, you will communicate that in your asking. And it will cause a blockage to your receiving. So this 'clean-up' is not about making yourself more deserving to the Universe but rather for you to feel deserving so that you can attract and manifest.

Draw the distinction between desire and yearning.

Know that you deserve the thing you desire and believe with implicit faith that you can and will have it.

You are worthy and deserving of your desires. This is the truth. Your parents brought you into this world through an act of love and you are here with many gifts and attributes to share with your family, friends, community and the world. Following your heart's Desire is the same as living God's will, when you listen to your inner self and wisdom, you are actually carrying out God's intention.

You are deserving of love, laughter, abundance, joy, forgiveness, your dreams, success, peace, pleasure, health, healing, sunshine, compassion, acceptance, giving and receiving, friends, nature or comfort and opulent experiences, kindness, beautiful experiences and scrumptious meals and respect. Yes, you deserve all this, and more! If you feel you are not deserving of all this but instead you feel you deserve punishment or to be abused and treated badly, then you will get that, too. If that is what you are manifesting in your life, you have to realise that it is what you are accepting and tolerating in your life.

Bad situations and bad people can come into your world, but if you choose to stay there then you are accepting and allowing it to continue. That is a sure sign of what you feel you deserve.

Thinking Pink Declaration Exercise
My Personal Declaration

Once you have come this far in the book, you will have a decently clear idea of what you most want and that should go into your declaration. Once again, what do you want? What do you really really want? Is it love, honesty, truthfulness, freedom, to be cared for, confidence, strength, adventure, inspiration, to inspire, creativity? Sit with this for a few minutes and choose the words that you feel connected with. Carry this thought with you and do not worry if you cannot come up with your declaration yet. By the end of the book, you can look at this again.

I found my declaration over a decade ago and I have lived by it since. It has guided me to make decisions, face adversity, change my posture and lift my mood whenever I have needed to. If the people around me through my actions notice the essence of the four words in my personal declaration, my way of being and my writing, then I know that I am living by it. If they do show up in a speech for me, perhaps on my next big birthday and in my Eulogy, then I will have lived my entire life by my declaration. That is the power of this declaration. People will feel it and see it without you having to say it to them. It usually stems from what we want and think we do not have, declare the feeling you so want and make it yours. If you want love, love, if you want truth, be authentic, if you want to be cared for, be caring.

This is how a personal declaration should look.

'I am a caring, responsible and strong man.'
'I am a strong, loving, independent and authentic woman.'
'I am a loving, fun, confident and inspiring man.'
'I am a healthy, honest and caring woman.'

4

Moving Forward

Things won are done, joy's soul lies in the doing.
— William Shakespeare (Troilus and Cressida)

Many cultures and religions have taught us that it is selfish or greedy to have desires. We have been conditioned to think that wanting too much for ourselves is wrong. The paradox is that without desire, we cannot be successful. When we are striving for desires that will give us what we want and enrich the lives of the people around us directly or indirectly, the Universe works with us to manifest it.

It does not need to be an altruistic desire, like one to save the world. Even the shopaholic whose only desire is to be able to buy the entire accessories department at Harrods is enriching the lives of everyone, from the saleswoman behind the counter to the families of the workers in the factories in China. Think of where the handbag or belt came from, the raw-materials and labour that went into it, then the logistic companies that went into getting them to you, the employees of the shipping company and the container yards, to each fork lift driver, warehouse pickers and packers to the lady serving you who's salary supports her children's education and puts food on the table. When you are Plugged In, you will be able to see the helicopter view of this instead of just looking at shopping as a mundane trivial act. You are circulating Universal energy.

As there are varying degrees of selfishness and not all are evil, in some ways being selfish is also taking responsibility for your 'self' and your life. Taking ownership of yourself and creating the life you desire is ultimately more satisfying than seeing yourself as a victim to circumstance and powerlessly blaming others for the state of your life.

When we decide what we truly desire, we start the process. The instant we take the nascent steps towards attaining it, the chain of events and ripple effect that is put into motion, just from our intention, declaration and action, is phenomenal and much larger than you or me.

Following it through by taking concrete steps towards attaining that desire will fuel the Universe even more and bring us closer to our goal.

How to achieve your desires

Evaluate your desire and, if necessary, break it down into small achievable goals. Take some small steps in preparation for that new life and then behave as if you have already achieved your desires. For instance, if your dream is to travel, buy new travel luggage in your favourite colour. Or if you intend to lose some weight, buy some gym clothes even when you are not sure how you are going to lose the weight or what exercise you are going to start with. In a way, you are *pretending* until it becomes real, like the age-old adage goes, 'fake it till you make it'. The only difference is that it is not fake as these are the steps to achieving your desires.

When we start to *feel* the joy of already having achieved our desires, we will radiate the emotions and vibrations that are necessary to attract positivity into our lives. Your positive expectations are what will make your desires a reality. The Universe responds to the way we feel. When we feel positive and happy, we emanate positive vibrations and these vibrations in turn attract more positive situations into our lives. Like attracts like.

Let us understand it through Kyrra's determination.

Kyrra had a mental image of herself living the lifestyle she desired. She saw herself travelling extensively, staying in five-star hotels and having a slim and healthy body. In her fantasy and imagination, she envisioned herself sitting in her tracksuit working from home most days or getting in and out of luxury cars, her feet clad in sexy high heels. She also imagined herself sipping cocktails with a sparkling diamond ring on her ring finger. This mental image encompassed many of her heart's deepest desires. When she played back the images, accompanied with a soundtrack which hummed Johnny Nash's insanely famous 'It's gonna' be a bright, bright sun-shiny day,' she could not help but smile. Kyrra envisioned herself smiling and throwing her head back in laughter frequently. And in reality, while she practiced this visualisation exercise, she felt these feelings in her chest and was often flooded by the joy. These emotions accompanied her thoughts and attracted the reality into her life. Not long after she had shifted her energies and started practicing the visualisation process regularly—feeling the joy as if she was already living her dream—she was swept off her feet in love and her career, too, took off, enabling her to lie in hammocks while she celebrated her success with her fiancé.

Aligned action

Most of us are wrapped up in the day-to-day of our lives and, like a hamster, we run and run as fast as we can, panting and puffing, making noise running within this wheel, only to see that everything is the same, in the same place. Nothing has changed. Therefore, from time to time, it is necessary to stop and ask ourselves what we want and if we are 'running' towards our dreams and, like the poor little hamster, going nowhere!

A feeling of dissatisfaction arises from feeling 'I don't have what I want.' The reality is that some of us do not know what that is. Therefore, we go through our lives feeling unhappy and dissatisfied. We have a fleeting wish—a glimpse of what we think we want and then go off in pursuit of it, only to feel just as bored and discontent even after achieving it. This can be likened to a hungry toddler who is given a pacifier instead of milk to suckle on, satisfying his need to suckle but not his hunger.

Underlying compelling desires

One of the things that stop people from wanting to set goals is that they feel they never achieve them. This is not true, all your desires are manifested, all your goals are achieved, it is that they were achieved on a level that you are not aware of. For example, you may set a goal to lose weight and want to be say, 60 kilograms from 75. However, you get to 63 and cannot get any further. What you have to do is go through the process of what you did accomplish along the way. Perhaps you developed good eating habits, joined a gym and made a workout buddy and started fitting into that discarded pair of old jeans. And then you stopped losing the weight.

What this could mean is that all you wanted to do was to fit into your jeans. That is where your magic was! So once your subconscious realised this, it aborted the goal. This could be true with so many other types of goals, especially when the underlying desire is to gain the appreciation or recognition of someone, or to prove something to yourself and once we get there, our emotional attachment to the goal dissolves. So you did not fail in manifesting, you just lost interest when the true desire came to be. This is great, because you can then celebrate your achievements and move on to different desires.

The beauty is that while we pursue our declared desires, we uncover their underlying significance. It is not just the tangible results that matter, but the growth in the journey. Let us take the famous 'lose weight' one. The underlying reasons behind this goal are often so much more than meets the eye. Someone who wants to become lighter and slimmer may have personal confidence and self-esteem linked to it, which often boils down to feeling 'good enough' and being loved.

These underlying wants are not obvious and often stay hidden in our subconscious. Trust that when you come up with desires you want to declare the path will unfold itself and along the way all the underlying wants will be experienced as well. Imagine that you have keyed in your destination into your navigation system and the computer has calculated the optional routes you could take, but along the way all the detours, scenic options and pit stops you discover are possibly opportunities for these underlying desires to be met. Plug In and trust that your inner guiding system knows better than you but that the path has to be travelled personally by you.

Taking action towards your desires

Now that you have set your goals and identified your desires, you are ready to first, take action despite all the odds, and second, trust the Universe implicitly. I cannot emphasise this enough. We have to phrase the goal in positive language and in the present tense, as if you already have it.

Life is always chaotic and busy. We have full lives with lots of things going on. How many times have you seen a new idea or a concept, which has become the next best thing since 'sliced bread', and thought, 'I thought of that!!' The only difference is the other person acted on his thoughts and you didn't. When you wait for things to be just right, you often lose the opportunity completely. You snooze, you lose. Life is what happens when you are too busy planning the details.

We have all read that the mind is infinitely powerful and that everything springs from our thoughts. But thought without action remains just that, a thought, it has only the potential of becoming something but until you add some action to the thought, it remains stagnant. It is something that has the possibility of being, but not being until a time in the future. Action is what makes it present and brings the energy into the Now.

Think about swimming, it is done in a horizontal position which is not natural for many people. Most beginners feel disorientated when floating on the water. They sometimes feel like they are drowning. The thing to do in the water, though, is to keep moving. When you stop kicking and paddling your legs and moving your arms, you stop swimming. Having said that, the more relaxed you are the easier it is to stay afloat. Taking action is not about being hectic, it is about taking steps towards your desires while having complete faith that you will get there gracefully and with ease. Doubt causes us to panic, and as in the swimming pool, when you panic, you cannot swim.

'I don't *feel* like it,' is a common chant we often say to ourselves or to others when we're tired, not in the mood, or simply procrastinating. *The time is not right. I am not ready. When I have this project done. When I have settled this case. When I have paid off that bill or that debt. When I lose weight. When I have renovated the house.* If you are going to wait for everything to be perfect, you will procrastinate too much and never set your desires into motion. Never! Take the first step, whatever that may be. Take it now. The time is now, or never! When you know you need to get to the other end of a room, you walk there, without thinking of the mechanics of putting one foot in front of the other. You simply take the first step and before you know you are there. Similarly, take the first step towards your desire.

Use Newton's 'Law of Inertia' which states that, 'An object in motion stays in motion while an object at rest stays at rest until an external force acts upon it.' Think of the desire as the object and your mind as the force that has to put it in motion.

Have you had a project/work you wanted to start/do but postponed, saying you will start it when this or that happens?

When I am not that busy
When the baby is older
When the house is ready
When I get a new computer
After I lose weight
When I have money
When the family stops fighting

When this investment matures
When I am ready
As Rabbi Hillel—the famous Jewish Rabii (c.110BCE-10CE)—so aptly said: If not now, when?

Everything that starts now, starts. It is conceived and once you start something it has only one thing to do thereafter, grow. If we wait for turmoil to settle, we will never start.

Have you liked a man or a woman, but felt you were not in the right place? Well, here is the news, the right time and place is *Now*. When two should cross paths, they choose whether to walk alongside or to deviate. That choice is made *Now*. If the desire is to be in a loving, intimate, committed relationship with someone who you connect with, whether or not there is any turmoil, you shoot the arrow.

While you wait for the first signs of manifestation, be patient. Imagine you are in a fine dining restaurant and have placed your order. It is now being carefully prepared in the kitchen by the professional chefs and although some things may need a little slow-cooking, you can be sure your food will arrive on the table in front of you soon enough. In the meantime just be ready and grateful to receive, especially since the joy and gratitude will attract it to you quicker. It is already yours in the spiritual realm and may take some time to manifest in the physical realm for you to see. Believe that it is already *yours* and you will get that email, phone call, idea—and everything shifts into gear to help you achieve the goals you desire. But remember, until then it is crucial at the stage to trust and to be grateful.

Having faith and knowing the manifestation of your desires is on its way to you is different from waiting for everything to be perfect before you start working towards them. Having the motivation to start, driven by your own compelling desire is what puts everything in motion. The law works by giving to the receiving hands. For as long as you are going to start something, you are always 'going to' rather than having 'started it'. The law does not respond to the future tense. The only tense it comprehends is the present continuous tense. Taking action now, however small, will create a vessel, a pot for our desires to fall into. Imagine driving around in a convertible with the top down when it is raining cash. Taking action is opening the top and letting the Universe know you are ready to receive, with your Heart Wide Open.

Like an archer on the battlefield, he focuses, aims and shoots. As expected, cannons are going off around him, but he remains calm and in no way perturbed.

Life is always full of turmoil, but when you are focused on your desired outcome, you will be able to see the target and shoot for it.

Mental or circumstantial chaos can be noisy and distracting, focusing on the 'target' amid the noise and chatter, the drama and perceived pain, will perpetuate more beauty in your life. Then one day, you get that unexpected email, phone call, idea, etc and then suddenly, everything changes. When you experience this, you will know that you have shifted the energy, creating a space for more beautiful opportunities.

Haven't you heard the phrase 'when it rains, it pours'? That is what you will experience! Everywhere you look, good things will be happening. This is when you will hear people saying, *'You have taken off'*, *'You are on a roll!'*

Haven't you noticed when you start opening your mind and heart to people, more people come into your life? You connect to the people that make all the difference in your life.

Once you decide to take the first step toward fulfilling your desires, the universe magically rearranges everything to make it all start happening for you.

— *Malti Bhojwani*

Your inbuilt GPRS

Follow your instincts to do what you *want* to do. When you are faced with opportunities and alternatives or choices, get clear with your personal declaration, values and your desires and just do what you want to do. Taking small steps towards your desires activates the magic. Keeping your values and your desires in mind, wait for inspired action and you will know what to do! It is like going to shop when you have a shopping list in mind. You will find what you are looking for. It is the same with what to do next, you will know. If you can't think of anything at all to do, don't just do what you think you should do, or what you think will bring you instant gratification or what you think is expected of you. Do what you *want* to do. Trust that in doing so you will be on your path and the directions will recalculate themselves—just like it does when you key in an address in your satellite navigation or GPRS and then start driving your car. Without moving at all, it can't tell you where to go, so act you must. The path is lit with the first step.

Piecing it together

Trust the Universe Implicitly. This means trusting that everything is as it should ideally be. Perfect. Even the things that seem bad or wrong. Things that look like mistakes or lost opportunities are perfect, too.

\# *Be clear on the compelling desire.* Know what you don't want to discover what you really want. Be clear and specific about what you want. Clarifying exactly what you want often, what we want so much is a feeling rather than a material possession or a situation—most of us want to be rich because we want fame and freedom, we want a relationship because we want to feel loved and appreciated, we want to lose weight because we want to feel accepted and attractive.

\# *Identify the wants, and the underlying desires that drive these wants.* Striving to get the best out of life is not only natural, it's achievable. The hard part is finding the motivation to overcome your stalling. Setting smart goals is easy, making resolutions are common every first day of New Year, signing up with a gym is too easy, the challenging thing is sticking to the plan. Make the declaration to stay committed to act in spite of habit, laziness, boredom or any other excuse we can conjure up. Everyone's dreams are different, but you would be amazed how far you can get with a commitment, a practical plan and just starting.

\# *Ask for it. Check your feelings.* Make sure that you feel deserving. If there is any action you can take at this point to help you feel more deserving—do it. Rephrase your goals and your desires in the positive. This tool itself can change your life. For example, instead of saying I want to lose some weight, go for a positive goal like wanting to fit into that red dress, or those jeans from 1997. Make your to-do list now and list at least six things that you can do this week that will be the first step to manifesting your desires. For example if you want to learn to drive, call up a driving school tomorrow, if you want to shed some weight, commit to exercising and changing your food plan starting tomorrow. There are no excuses, only results.

\# *Check ecology.* Make sure it is something that resonates well with you, is for your highest good and the good of everyone involved.

\# *Trust you are this huge magnet attracting this desired outcome into your life.* Visualise it all coming to you and then sit back, be patient and calm and allow it to happen. It will.

5

Replacing Negativity

I am always at a loss at how much to believe of my own stories.
— *Washington Irving*

Change your negative thoughts before they manifest rather than after.

What is the truth and what is a lie? Think of a few lies you have told in your life. This may be challenging, because often we say misleading things to others and to ourselves and we want to believe them so much that we end up fooling ourselves in the process.

When I was an obese teenager in Sydney, I was desperate to lose weight. Plus, the usual methods of watching my food and doing regular exercise were not giving me the results I wanted fast enough, so I responded to a 'lose-weight-fast' advertisement and signed up for a slimming treatment that involved body wraps and fat mobilisation. I was scared to tell my parents where I was going for two hours three times a week and where I was spending the money, so I lied to them that I signed up at an exclusive gym. Unfortunately, one afternoon, as I got up from their treatment bed, I felt light-headed and I passed out, falling on the ground and piercing my back on the edge of the stainless steel bed frame.

One lie leads to a dozen more to cover up, as you know, so I had to say that I fell off the treadmill at the gym. I am telling this story here because only a few days ago, over 25 years later, I was on a treadmill and as I was going to get off, I had that light-headed feeling again and my body went into fear. I noticed myself thinking, 'Oh-no! Be careful, you have fallen off a treadmill before and hurt yourself.' I then recalled falling off a treadmill when, in actuality, that had never happened. Until then, I had never fallen off a treadmill in reality. I had told the lie so many times, I had conjured up the image of it in my head and believed it to have really happened. This is the very phenomena that prevents a lie-detector from working on some people.

See, I had told the lie so many times 25 years ago that I believed it to be the truth. When we lie, it is not just the words we use, but to be believable we can conjure up a mental image in our heads to support the lie and then the feelings that go with the lie.

This example was one of a lie that involved a true past experience I remember, however what you have to notice is the little lies that are not so easily distinguishable from the truth. The ones that deceive us the most are the ones we tell ourselves about how things are.

I used the word *lie* to illustrate my story to show how powerful our beliefs can be. Another word for lies could be stories. Yes, stories about our past that we repeat to people in our lives. As we do that, we perpetuate, repeat and each time we do, we are making that story more and more real. Soon it will be committed to our memory and our bodies in a way that makes it the 'truth'. But is it, really?

Story Telling Exercise

Tell your story, the short version from childhood to now. Pause from reading for a few moments and tell the story to yourself. 'I was born in Singapore in 1971 and I was embarrassingly fat at school and everyone used to tease me and…the boy I had a crush on when I was thirteen called me a 'fat lump of s*^t', then I got married to the guy who didn't think I was so fat and ugly and I turned vegetarian and gave up alcohol before even trying it…'

Tell *your* story as if it was the saddest story ever told. Slouch your shoulders, speak slowly and speak in a low monotonous tone. Now tell the same story as if it were a script in a comedy show. Same story, but it sounded different I am sure. So which story is the truth, which one is a lie? You can try this with the story of your relationships, your business or your job. Tell the story about why one relationship or business failed and then tell the same story from the view of how it was an experience that brought you to where you are today, with your new learning. Notice the difference in your body position, your breathing and your tone: notice how differently you felt each time you told the story in a different mood.

Most of us get into a habit of telling the story a certain way, to invoke a certain emotion. We want the listener to empathise with us, to like us and see us in a good light, always. Or we could be looking to victimise ourselves and get sympathy from the listener. Remember 90 per cent of the time, the 'listener' is us. We are telling the story the way we want to hear it. Wisdom is knowing which one to listen to at which moment.

This is a double-edged sword, as we have told so many stories and we believe them to be true and these stories then come back to create the same fears and emotion in our present day when triggered, just like my real fear of falling off the treadmill.

Given there are no truths about our past, they are all interpretations that we had of certain incidents from the view of how we were looking at them at the time, we can retell the story so it is empowering. Everything in this book is about making the choices that will make you a better *'manifester'* of your desires.

One of the biggest enemies of being able to manifest is wanting to be right about everything. Every chapter in this book will invite you to practice a new way of being, which will contradict with how you have always been. Most of us have an inane need to know and understand every single detail, the invitation here is to trust the process and practice it.

Our stories become self-fulfilling; we will always live up to the story. So make it a desired one. Imagine if the famous Indian tennis player Sania Mirza told herself that she could not be a WTA Champion (Women's Tennis Association) because of her race or her gender.

Imagine if Thomas Edison believed his impaired hearing would prevent him from learning.

Imagine if Oprah Winfrey believed that she was 'unfit for TV' when she was fired from one of her earlier jobs as a reporter.

What if Richard Branson kept telling himself that he was incapable because of his Dyslexia growing up?

The stories we tell ourselves and the meanings we give to these stories dictate where we go and what we create in our experience.

I had my share of negative beliefs. Soon after my divorce, I went around with two strong beliefs. First, 'I was not good enough,' and second, 'all men are jerks.' This had nothing to do with my ex-husband who is still a friend and family to me. However, what I positively did was I attracted a true jerk into my experience soon after I was single again. He met me the day he was released from prison where he was incarcerated for larceny and assault. Of course I did not know this at the time. All the signs were there, secretive phone conversations, innuendo and looks from people around, someone even came to warn my parents about him and coincidentally ended up dead a few weeks later; but blinded by his charming good looks, suave suits and his promise to me of a better life for my daughter and myself, I was oblivious to the way he treated me. But then I had the broken record playing underneath saying, 'You are not good enough for someone who will treat you better!' The record got even more scratched because by then I had the added track playing that said, 'You are a divorced Indian woman.' So, I allowed him to treat me badly, I allowed him to swindle and con me of all the money I had and didn't have, sell my jewellery to help him open a business in my name which hurt my family, while he gambled all the shop's takings on a roulette table in the casinos in Sydney and got me close to bankruptcy. My daughter sensed it from the start, but I did not see it. I thought it was normal for her to have reservations about her mother marrying again and bringing a stepfather into her life. In fact it was that experience that kept me from remarrying all those years. The only time that I reconsidered that decision was after my daughter had gone to college. I sought advice and battled with the conflict in my mind, and believed I was doing the right thing for both of us at the time. I was in my mid-twenties and the hope for a family of my own again was intensely inviting to me. My self-deprecating thoughts allowed me to stay with this man and accept his behaviour because I didn't think I deserved to be in a healthier relationship.

As I said, we are always manifesting and just as easily as you can manifest wonderful desires into your life, you can also manifest your worst nightmares.

It was indeed painful, in every way, for my daughter, my family and myself. However even with him, I learnt so much. Most of all, I realised how lowly I thought of myself and how depleted my self esteem was at that time. I thought that being with someone like him was what I deserved and I accepted it. It was only after I went through years of self-awareness that I understood the power of forgiving and only after I allowed myself to forgive my self, ask for forgiveness from my daughter and forgive him in my own heart and release the anger I had for him and only when I gave up the hope that he would ever one day return all that he took from me that I was able to truly let go and live again. This process took longer that it needed to, for back then I didn't know what I know now.

Remixes

Have you heard remixes of your favourite songs from the 70s, 80s and the 90s?

A remix can change the feel, the emotional charge and the meaning of the song. Musicians and DJs scratch and reharmonise music by adding new elements, beats and at times voice to change the song and yet maintain the underlying tune and lyrics, keeping the original still recognisable. When you rescript your old stories that no longer serve you, look at it as creating the 'remix' version of your stories.

Going back to the exercise, write a new story about three of the most important phases of your past. It could be your childhood, schooling, a past relationship or a business or career path that did not go the way you wanted. This time, write the story only looking at *why* it was so good for you. If I could remix my rendezvous with the dashing con-artist, to something that I can laugh at today, I am sure you can remix your horror stories as well.

Also try to hunt for the facts rather than the judgements that you made at the time. I called myself obese, my schoolteachers and the report card called me obese and I told people that I ate like a pig, but in fact it was all relative. In any other country, I would have been simply chubby or plump. When I rewrote that part, I said, 'I was 58 kilograms and I loved my food.' Already, I changed the way I saw myself back then and I changed the language I used around the story. The easiest way to rewrite your story is to start each paragraph with 'I am so grateful that...' Do this with what you would call your big stories first and then you will be able to 'rewrite' all stories to make them empowering rather than disempowering.

We have stories that don't have a leg to stand on. Some of you may know them as negative personal assessments, limiting beliefs, underlying negative commitments or even the truth based on your past. They are all essentially the same thing, the negative self-talk that we burn our own ears with. It is so common and so 'natural' that sometimes we do not even notice it or 'hear it', but it is doing its job and you will feel it in your body. It will show up in your actions and then your results if you allow it to control.

Some examples of what we say to ourselves, 'I can't do this', 'I will never be successful'. While writing this book, I had my own voice that sometimes said, 'You will never finish the book on time, who are you kidding?'

If you remember the statement in an earlier chapter, 'Would you rather be right or happy?'

Think of these negative thoughts and stories as a parasite or virus, they are doing their job but, unfortunately, their survival is the death of your dreams. They, too, have a purpose which is also self-preserving. We started believing some things and these lines, long ago, helped us to protect ourselves from disappointment and getting hurt. So do not hate your old beliefs or the voice in your head, instead, notice them and shoo them off when what they say to you is no longer empowering. The bad news is that they will never leave you alone for long; the good news is now that you have started noticing these, train yourself to tell the new stories to you, the ones that will empower you rather than paralyse you.

The negative chatter needs to be replaced too. In Neuro Linguistic Programming (NLP), the old negative chatter is just a neurological pathway that you use out of habit. You need to create new pathways so you can practice using the alternative routes more often. And with enough practice, slowly, those will become a new habit. This does not mean the negative stuff disappears forever, unfortunately it remains because you have used them so often, all your life up till now you have etched deep pathways in your mind. They have become a kind of a default option, only now you have another option; you have an alternative that you never knew you had before. So once you have rewritten the script and replaced your negative statements about yourself and life and how the Universe works, with empowering ones, then practicing to use the new ones will etch the fresh pathways, making it a more familiar path.

Not entertaining the negative chatter is great, but it is impossible to do unless you give yourself new scripts. You need to become like a sentry or watchman of your chatter and notice each disempowering one when they come up and then replace them with empowering ones. If I asked you now, 'Whatever you do, DO NOT think of a blue ball', what is the image you conjured up in your head? A blue ball! You cannot *not* think of something, without first thinking of it. Can you? If I asked you to think of a yellow ball now, you can. But asking you to NOT THINK of a blue ball is rather impossible. If you apply this basic analogy to all your negative stories, lies and self-talk, you will see why you have not been able to *not* think negative thoughts, the crucial step of replacing the stories, lies and negative beliefs is what you may have missed. After a broken relationship, your voice would say, 'Don't think of Sandy'. How can you not think of Sandy without first thinking of Sandy? Your self-talk means well, it just needs to be trained to use language effectively to help you manifest your desires instead of perpetuating your current results.

The most dangerous effects of these negative stories and thoughts are the feelings that these evoke in you. Negative and sad feelings of doubt and worry lower your attraction power of what you want. This is why they can be disempowering. And this is why you need to find tricks and ways to change the way you feel in that moment. The quickest way to do that is to think a happy thought.

By watching the mind, observing your thoughts and maintaining concentration on the breath you will be able to control it and master it with patience. Cultivate the routine of monitoring your thoughts and the words you use repeatedly. What are you thinking? What percentage of time do you spend in positive attraction mode and what percentage of time do you spend in negative thought patterns?

Your negative thoughts are not bad, they are great because when you think and feel worried, anxious or fearful it means that you are thinking thoughts that are not aligned with your desires. This is great because it is an immediate signal to you to be reminded of what you want. You are more clear about what you do want when you know rather strongly what you are afraid of and what you don't want. Feeling worrisome and complaining is a good trigger to move from doubt to positive expectations.

So they are there to remind you and alert you that you are not aligned; however, you must not allow yourself to stay in that feeling for long. You have to, and I cannot stress this enough, *you have to think positive and happy thoughts, even if they are unrelated, to change the way you are feeling.*

Feeling good about anything means you are connected and Plugged In just as feeling badly and complaining means that you have un-plugged yourself. When you complain about anything, however tiny or huge they may seem to you, all you are doing is adding more negative vibrations and hence inviting more of the same experience and in a higher intensity. While editing this book, my Mac Book started to act up and instead of practicing my own principles, instead of Plugging In, being grateful and thinking happy thoughts, I complained and allowed it to grow, and guess what, the next morning, I had internet connection issues and I had to travel around the streets of Mumbai in a rickshaw trying to fix it and then guess what, my website and server crashed and I could not access my emails at all. Luckily, at some point, I noticed the cool wind on my face, while I sat in the rickety three-wheeler, as it was a beautiful time in Mumbai, with temperatures of 20 degrees in the afternoon. I noticed the bright blue sky and I was able to finally turn my energies to much more pleasant things than my technical-issues.

Look for reasons to feel good. Good memories from the past, pleasant things in your now and fantasies you have about your future. Do you remember play-acting and fantasising when you were a kid? I remember always dreaming that I was a princess from a fairy tale or a heroine from one of the Hindi movies I watched. I am not sure what boys fantasised about in their younger years, I think it must be cars, rockets and kissing girls, perhaps? We could spend hours doing so, this is what you need to do now, even if it sounds childlike or ridiculous to you, do it. Find any way to feel good, especially when you are annoyed, worried or anxious.

Experience the joie de vie—joy of life, in every opportunity and moment you can.

Your negative worries will visit you time and again, but you should thank them for reminding you that you are not Plugged In. When your connection is weak, the bars are low, or you are in a low-signal territory—quickly pick any positive and happy thought and change the way you are feeling.

There is nothing good about feeling bad even when small events happen, nothing will be undone if you are feeling sad. Find something good and ride that thought instead. Do not join the masses in feeling sorry or reacting habitually and typically to situations, most of our reactions are just habit or societal norms. If you spill something, you get upset, when caught in traffic you complain, if someone is late you get irritated, there is no need for you to indulge in feeling bad even for a few moments. Change the thought and change the feeling. Confidence and faith is expecting positive outcomes no matter what, not only when it is convenient.

Quickly choose one pleasurable thought to switch to and if you can't think of anything happy, be grateful for what you have in that moment.

A couple of years ago, I was feeling like my life was in limbo and I was using phrases 'in the interim' and 'in the meantime' a lot. In fact my daughter, then only eighteen, pointed it out to me. I realised for as long as I used those words, I would continue to be in a space of 'in the meantime'— waiting for someone else to do something or for something to happen magically before I would start living my life and be in the *Now*.

It was a challenging task, as it had become almost a habit (you know when you learn a new word or hear an expression being used somewhere and use it all the time?). So I had to consciously correct myself and choose my words carefully to use more 'present' words. Doing that, changing my language in the words I uttered and the words I used in my self-talk, made the shift from 'in the interim' to *Now* for me, and guess what? Manifestation can only occur in the *Now*, in the present moment. The entire Universe is happening only in this moment!

You inner voice does not only have negative chatter. If you look at all the areas of your life that are going well, you will notice the chatter around those areas are indeed utterly positive and empowering. Someone who is fit will have positive health and fitness chatter about their bodies and health. Someone who has many friends and is social, would have chatter that affirms that.

Words are not enough

How do you make yourself feel good when you have negative thoughts, anxiety or sadness owing to a lost love, an illness or the fear of not having money? Well, perpetuating on those thoughts will only attract more sadness, anxiety, lack into your life, so you don't have a choice if you want to be happy.

The easiest way to trick yourself into vibrating positive feelings is to use your memories and your fantasies and your dreams and desires. It IS as easy as that!

Every time and I mean every single time you notice a sad, disempowering, scary, anxious, helpless thought cross your mind, train yourself to switch it. Just like you would turn on a light switch! Switch it! Have in your 'reserves' those positive thoughts which will make you feel good, even if it were for a few moments. It is enough. As you make a habit of always switching to a positive, feel good thought and you actually experience the 'good-feelings', even if they are *naughty thoughts* that bring you there and make you smile, you are vibrating on a higher level that can only attract more positivity into your life.

I have been deeply inspired by authors Lynn Grabhorn and by Napolean Hill and both have shown me the infinite power of feeling as opposed to just thinking. The vibrational changes happen when we feel good.

The actual 'how-to' is simple, think of something that makes you feel good, then while you are feeling those good sensations, imagine yourself 'flowing out' these good vibrations. Imagine all this good energy or light beaming out from your heart. This flowing out will make you change your breathing and open your chest. This openness is what invites more in and what allows you to connect with the Universal energies around you.

Invitation

Create your personal pleasure list.

Pleasure lists: This is an exceptionally useful exercise to help you feel good whenever, on demand, on tap. List ten things (activities) for four separate categories that give you joy and pleasure. There are four categories: Cheap Thrills 10s, Easy 20s, Lavish 50s and Decadent 100s.

\# *Cheap Thrills 10s*: These are things that are very easy for you to indulge in; indulge in them as often as you like as they require little time or money from you.

These are not too indulgent. And frequent use of these should not interfere with any of your other health or work goals.

For me this list may include:

smelling a rose;
sending a message to a friend;
having a cup of herbal tea.

\# *Easy 20s*: Things that take some time and maybe money. These are quite easy as well, but you will need to schedule them in, make time and spend money for them. You probably would participate in moderation as they have a higher 'price' attached to them.

For some this list may include:
enjoying a glass of white wine;

slow leisurely love-making, or fantasizing of;

calling or Skyping with a close friend or family—this takes up time;

taking a long bath with scented foam and oils;

going for a Pilates or Yoga class (It is amazing when your pleasure lists start to include things you used to consider as 'work, tasks, or exercise').

\# *Lavish 50s:* 50s are things that take up more time and money and may need a little bit of preplanning.

This list may include:

buying a new pair of shoes, a dress, a perfume, make up;

going for a massage or facial;

taking a friend out for a nice dinner at a new restaurant perhaps and ordering a bottle of Champagne or even inviting a few friends over for dinner.

\# *Decadent 100s:* Lastly, list 10 things that use up more time and money and perhaps need even more planning and reshuffling of work, family, people and commitments.

For me this list may include:

travelling for pleasure;

exploring a new business venture;

learning a new skill;

contributing and committing to a social cause;

buying expensive gifts for friends;

indulging in an adventure sport, like sky-diving on hot-air ballooning;

Once you have finished listing ten activities for each of the four categories, you should have 40 activities in the list.

As soon as you finish this task, reward yourself immediately and go indulge in a couple of 10s right away, at least one 20 for today, schedule a 50 in for this weekend and start planning one of the 100s for the end of the year. As the days pass, you will notice that you will discover more and more activities that give you pleasure and you can come back to this list and fill them in the appropriate category. Just doing the exercise will create the 'option' or, as I have explained earlier, a new neurological path to take when you have a negative thought or when you are not feeling good.

Can you see how useful this list is going to be? Whenever you are having an off day, or you are feeling a little bored or disheartened, cheer yourself up by giving yourself some pleasure. It can be challenging to come up with pleasure activities when you are feeling horrible, though, but having done this exercise means that you have them on tap. You could also print this out and stick it up somewhere, as long as your pleasurable activities are things that you are comfortable with other people at home seeing.

Memories and fantasies

Even memories of past love or past experiences can bring out these higher vibrations. You want to visualise, remember or think of these thoughts till you actually start feeling the joy in your body and you experience a physiological change. One note on past love: it is sweet nostalgia when you have forgiven the person and the past, but if it still causes you pain then you have some forgiving yet to do so don't tap on those memories as yet.

Go back into your yesterdays, at times, and bathe your mind in the beautiful memories of past love. It will soften the influence of the present worries and annoyances. It will give you a source of escape from the unpleasant realities

— Napolean Hill, *Think And Grow Rich*

(Quoted here with consent from The Napolean Hill Foundation. www.naphill.org)

Remember: The worse we feel, the worse things get; the better we feel, the better everything gets.

How? Think of something nice, think of a dream you have coming true, think of sex, kisses, money, dancing, holidays, beaches, wind in your hair, look back at your pleasure list. CHANGE YOUR THOUGHT AND YOU WILL CHANGE THE WAY YOU FEEL—even if it only lasts for a few minutes; use those few minutes to FLOW those positive, happy, joyful feelings like energy out of you as if you are 'Sending' it to something. Imagine it to be like a laser pointer while you are beaming this positive vibration outwards. How we feel is how we vibrate, and how we vibrate equals to how we manifest.

Learn to honour your emotions always by being willing to feel them. Of course, you may need to exercise some judgement over how and when you express them.

When you start thinking and feeling happy, you will find that you can imagine and think of more and more happy and fun thoughts, fantasies for the future or memories from the past, hopes and desires. Once you fill your head with positive and pleasant thoughts, there will be less and less 'space' for anything negative.

You can't think about something you don't want and expect to get what you want. That is absurd, remember the blue ball?

Eulogy

The most powerful story you can write and rewrite is your eulogy. Think about how long you would like to live, and then if you can imagine yourself as old and that you have died. Imagine that your grandchild or closest friend decides to take the podium to say a few words about you and your life. What would you like them to say? If you keep going the way you are now, changing nothing about you and your life, what would they say? What would you like to be remembered for/ as? What do you want your eulogy to say? Write a paragraph and keep it safely in your sacred space. This is one of the most powerful stories about the future that you can write *Now*. I keep mine in my altar.

Invitation

Put the book down for a few moments and do this now. All you need to write is a short paragraph.

You would start it with your name;

Malti Bhojwani was a loving, strong, fiercely independent and incredibly authentic woman. Anyone who had the pleasure of spending time with her was diffused with her loving and positive way of being. She lived on her own rules and allowed herself to be vulnerable throughout as she always wanted to feel and extract as much as she could out of any experience...

Pick three areas of your life, relationships, work and finances and health.

Write down two old stories or statements that you have made around each of these areas. For example, 'All relationships are hard' or 'Money does not come easy'.

Next, look at your results in these three areas and then notice how your statements almost predicted the results. If the results are awesome, that is fabulous and chances are your stories or statements around them are fabulous as well. If your results are not what you truly desire, then perhaps you should look at the stories or statements you had around them. Identify the ones that do not serve you and change these statements to powerful statements instead and you will start to manifest the desired results.

Negative talk

Do you ever begin a conversation with a complaint? Do you realise that every complaint is an affirmation of something you think you don't want in your life? Every time you get angry, you are affirming that you want more anger in your life. Every time you feel like a victim, you are affirming that you want to continue to feel like a victim. Remember how I perpetuated technical issues in my day? Positive affirmations are solutions that will replace whatever problem you might have. By repeating these affirmations over and over, you will be planting new seeds in the fertile soil of your subconscious mind and they will become true for you.

Buttons, triggers and our antagonists

As we have all heard, life is 10 per cent what happens to us and 90 per cent how we react to what happens to us. We have emotional relationships with certain words. This is also true of gestures—someone pointing a finger at you, a particular tone of voice or sound can 'rub you' the wrong way. I call these 'triggers' or 'buttons'. One of the greatest blocks to communication is that some words are emotionally charged. They are words that trigger an automatic emotional reaction within us. To use a trigger word in an argument—a word which can invoke a charge—can turn a discussion into a battle instantaneously. Words like 'never' and 'ever' also do the same.

We have at least one person in our life from time to time that pushes these buttons and triggers. One way to practice self-observation is don't question, 'Why it is so?' but rather question, 'Why do I have an issue with it being so?' Make a decision to list the endearing qualities of these people even if you don't experience them directly. This exercise can be challenging when you have a lot of negative emotions around these people but this is the only way through.

When a person flings a trigger word at us, or we at them, it is like we have shot or hosed them down. It usually causes them to go on the defensive and start flinging some back at us—or perhaps go into some other defensive mode, like, many women would panic or cry, whereas men would often shut down and retreat. As long as we are not willing to look for the cause behind our emotional relationship with a word we are still giving power to our past and whatever circumstance caused our emotional wound. These words bring out our underlying fears.

In simple terms, they are the things that you believe to be true about yourself and they then determine the basis for how you operate. It doesn't matter whether they are true or not, you believe *they are* true and so you make them your truth. Examples of some common ones are: *I am not good enough! No one loves me! Will I ever be loved for who I am?*

97

Am I a bad person? How do we break the pattern of reacting to triggers that activate these disempowering reactions instead of allowing us to respond from our authentic self and our true desires?

Searching for your identity is a process with no real destination. You will never be 'done' because you are always growing and changing. Living authentically and finding your identity involves dealing with your past and forgiving others. Noticing how we react to situations and the emotions that come up. These emotions give you the key to your underlying fears. After the reaction, stop and look at the feelings and doubts that come up in your mind when you find yourself afraid, panicking and resisting. When you find yourself willing and praying for a certain outcome, you will be able to face your deep-rooted underlying fear, which in my experience boils down to 'I am not good enough' for many of us. To help you discover these underlying fears, think about the trigger. We all have some triggers that fire off the process of negative emotions.

These fears include the ones we are consciously aware of, like the fear of spiders, for example, and some that we are not aware of, but these are the fears that cause us to react and feel a certain way about any given circumstance. The circumstance may be a problem or it may be an opportunity, our underlying fears will determine which. Increasing your self-awareness is a journey full of steps forward and regression. The next time you experience your body reacting to a trigger word, notice what it feels like and see if you can accept the feeling and choose a response instead of automatically reacting.

I have some trigger words that get me going. Mine include the words, 'allow', 'let', 'permission'. I resist authority and feel undermined when I feel it is being imposed on me. I am sure you do, too. It is that word or that assumption that often somebody else uses on you that sets you off—and often to an uncontrollable downward spiral where you are reacting and reacting, not realising that you are not reacting to just the current situation but you are reacting to the primary situation.—the first time you experienced these feelings and associated them with these triggers. The next time someone you are in any kind of relationship with pushes one of these buttons that triggers a negative emotion, stop, breathe and wait. Take time to respond rather than reacting in your conditioned, 'acceptable' way. When that trigger is fired, ask yourself: in what way you want to behave?

This can only be answered when we know who we are, who we want to be and what we want to have. Ask yourself, 'If I have already been through my journey and have already discovered this self, this beautiful self, how would he or she react in this situation? What outcome do I want here? What am I committed to creating here? To fulfil and give more supporting evidence to my old negative beliefs? Let this be another time I get to prove that—"All women are users", "All men are bastards", "There are no free rides", "People are always out to get me"—or do I want to create an outcome where I get to break the old patterns and reaffirm how I can live the life I desire and that I deserve to be happy?'

The key is to respond, based on the desired outcome rather than the limiting negative old belief. Practice makes perfect. Whenever we learn a new response to a predictable old pattern, we have to practice doing it deliberately. The difference is, when you do it on purpose, you can accelerate the learning. Otherwise, you are left to the slow learning that comes from repeating undesired behaviours over and over.

In the movie *Yes Man*, Jim Carrey's character Carl starts out as an extreme example of someone in the habit of reacting to every invitation or offer with a 'No'. No matter what opportunities come his way, no matter what someone may ask of him, Carl is pre-programmed and ready with an excuse about why he can't do it. In the movie, he is hypnotised into saying 'Yes' to everything. In the end, Carl finally learns how to say 'Yes' or 'No' authentically and with equal conviction, based on what he wants rather than an old negative belief that rendered him a prisoner of his own pre-programming. When we start to create a new habit of responding to the situations based on our truths, we are present, aware, receptive, vulnerable and open to the uncertainty of the next moment in time, being authentically who we are.

Unfortunately, despite best intentions the 'I'm not good enough' comes from our childhood. When you are around kids, realise that when a child comes up to you to show you something they have made or written, and out of the pure intention of being helpful you suggest more or offer feedback, you are clearly saying to the child that he or she is not good enough. This is what started and contributed to the entire negative language and beliefs that become barricades in our lives and we are so afraid of that being 'revealed'.

Happy talk

Your natural state is health and well-being and this is promoted and maintained by positive energy, positive thoughts, positive talk and good feelings. Negative energy is not good for you.

It causes tiredness, irritability, illness and disease. If it is in your system, it needs to be eliminated and kept out. The only way to keep it out is to replace it with positive thoughts and words. Simple? Let us see.

Because of the close connection between the mind and feelings, you have to choose and decide *Now* to think happy thoughts, use positive words and therefore feel good.

Watch what you say in all your conversations; choose to say only the happy stuff. Monitor yourself when you complain and change course. Have you noticed people who always update their social media sites and smart phones with complaints and negative statements? This is a sure way to attract more of that. Stop it now! There is no need to tell the world all the negative things you experienced. The experience may have lasted a minute or even an hour, and you sharing it is only going to create hours of attention on that. Why would you do that, knowing what you now know? Let it rest, the complaints. Think happy thoughts and talk happy words.

What you are doing is developing a positive attitude. You can sit there and expect everything to go wrong, or you can expect everything to go the other way. Based on the facts you have, let us just say that there is a 50 per cent chance of things going either way. Your expecting it to go the 'wrong' way is not going to make things any better for you. However, if you expect them to go the positive way no matter what, your positive expectations will help you be who you need to be, in order to do the stuff that will help you have what you desire.

A fabulous by-product of a positive attitude is that people around you notice the change in attitude and join in with positive thoughts of their own. Just like they join you when you are thinking negative ones. When I was ill last year and

I complained about my injury from my accident and my toothache from my cracked molar and my terribly sore throat, I attracted people around me who shared their aches and pains as well. Same way, when we think and say happy things, people will share their wins and joys as well.

Often, we don't want to share the cheer because we think people will scoff at us and say we are airy-fairy people from la-la land. No! Get over that need to 'fit in', it is far more empowering to be happy even if we end up looking 'foolish' to some. When you are going against the tide (most people are still quite happy being 'normal', 'sane', 'negative', they equate it with being practical)—when you are going against the tide, yes, it is a little more challenging. A great analogy I like to use is to imagine yourself walking on the beach towards the water with the waves coming in against you, it is far easier to do this when you are holding hands with someone or a group of people.

This is a habit that needs to be cultivated, it does feel unnatural at first, it can even feel silly; but the benefits will make it all worthwhile in the end. Happy thoughts and happy talk only. Remember the old song from *South Pacific*?

Happy talk, keep talkin' happy talk,
Talk about things you'd like to do.
You got to have a dream,
If you don't have a dream,
How you gonna have a dream come true?

Thinking is a habit. Habits take time and careful watching to replace. You can't stop thinking a certain way, you just have to start thinking a new way. So how do we develop healthy thinking habits? If a friend spoke to you the way you sometimes think to yourself when you are being your hardest with yourself, with horrible statements like 'How stupid am I! How stupid!', 'You never get it right', 'You always lose', and 'God you look awful in that', how long would you put up with a friend who spoke that way to you? So, why do you allow your own thoughts to tell you this garbage? The first step to forming a habit of thinking in an 'Empowering way' is to notice and become aware of the disempowering ways we have been thinking. The first thought is usually a neutral thought. Right after that first thought comes the myriad of subsequent thoughts, which are empowering or disempowering.

Negative thoughts pretend and attempt to protect us.

This is a story that a friend from my coach training shared with us.

When a zoo gains a new baby elephant, they chain one of his legs to a wooden pole allowing the young one only a short radius to explore and move around. The young elephant in his first few days of captivity tries to break free but soon learns that he can't, owing to the cuts his body suffers due to constricted movement. As he grows up into a mighty mammoth of a creature, the zookeepers do not change either the pole or the chain and if he only tries, the elephant can effortlessly yank his freedom by pulling at the chain, which at this stage would be more like pulling a toothpick out of the ground. However, it is his limiting belief (ingrained from his early experience) which has already taught him that it can't be done, so he remains in captivity despite his strength and power. Sounds familiar?

When you notice yourself having a disempowering thought:
\# Distract yourself with anything.

\# Dis-identify yourself from the thought. Imagine that the thought is outside of you and just like a movie running on a screen.

Clear the screen and play an empowering thought on purpose. Anything beautiful, positive, happy. Practice! Practice and practice! Keep doing this and it will slowly become a habit!

Invitation

Go through all your music, use your iTunes, CD collection, browse on the Internet and find ten songs that make you happy from the very first strains. In order to do this, you have to listen to the first few seconds of the number and then decide quickly if it has made you feel happy or not. Don't go for songs that make you feel emotionally sad, nostalgic or neutral, the emotion they should pump in you is that of joy. Make a personal playlist or CD of at least ten such songs. I have my current ten songs on my phone, my laptop and in a CD in my car.

Thinking Pink Exercise on—Achievements and Accomplishments

Start a list, handwritten or on your computer, iPad or Smartphone, of 50 of your accomplishments. You can think about your life chronologically and list everything that you consider an accomplishment.

Thinking Pink Exercise on—Antagonists

Use a small notebook and label the top of the page with the situation that you consider undesirable or a person that causes you irritation, resentment or upset. One page for each Antagonist or Antagonistic Situation and then list all the things that are absolutely great about them. Yes, do that. Ain't you feeling empowered already?

This can be challenging, but please trust the process.

My fall in 1989

(This is the list that went straight into my diary. I used it as an opportunity to make a permanent mental note of the following things. Read on!)

- can't think of anything great;
- truly can't for the life of me;
- all subsequent falls were taken more seriously to investigate for fractures;
- awfully careful on staircases in high heels;
- learnt the benefits of turmeric and milk;
- discovered my allergies to some pain killing drugs in a safe way that possibly saves me now.

My run in with the Con Artist

- learnt to eat oysters;
- learnt to play roulette;
- learnt to appreciate dessert wine;
- got to feel like I was in my own Hollywood action movie;
- learnt that all that glitters is not gold;
- learnt not to trust good looking men with my jewellery;
- learnt how much my family and friends loved me;
- discovered personal development which led to becoming a professional life coach and author.

6

Walking on Sunshine

People desire to separate their worlds into polarities of dark and light, ugly and beautiful, good and evil, right and wrong, inside and outside. Polarities serve us in our learning and growth, but as souls we are all.

— Joy Page

Have you ever been up on a hot-air balloon? Do you know the principle on which it moves when it is up in the sky? To describe it simply, air exists in layers and the different layers of air help it to move in different directions. Although there is no steering mechanism, the pilot can direct it by controlling which wind wave it rides. So simply by moving the balloon up or down, it will catch a different direction. You can liken this to learning how to allow and perhaps change your own way of being, instead of your direction, when you are moving towards manifesting your desires. You have your desires declared, you trust the universe and you are watching your words and your thoughts, now you have to learn to allow—which sometimes means not doing anything and sometimes may mean moving up and down on the same plane instead of trying to force yourself ahead.

Sometimes we get tired of trying (or barking up the wrong tree) so we persist and try harder, pushing boundaries and ignoring the stop signs. I have done this in relationships I obsessively wanted to work out, because I was so tired. When you are tired, instead of pushing harder, yearning, bargaining with the Universe, stop and rest. Physically, when we are tired we sit down, even lie down, take a breather, have a cup of tea or sleep etc. Have you ever been in an underground subway or train station where there are long escalators? Imagine that you are standing on a step on the escalator of your life. If you are not feeling Plugged In and you are unsure what to do next but you still insist on running as fast as you can, you will tire yourself out and end up feeling frustrated. Instead, sometimes the best thing to do is nothing, just like you could on an escalator, just stand peacefully and enjoy the billboards or hoardings on sides of the wall and relax. Notice the people who pass you by, absorb the signs and messages that cross your vision and trust that you will eventually get to the top feeling good, calm, rested and perhaps with new insights and intuition. There are times in your life when you are on the path that it is OK to just allow.

Up and down, forward and backward, left or right—these are all polarities. So are yin and yang, expanding and contracting, life and death and ebb and flow, to name a few. Like our lungs need to expand and contract and the sea has its ebbs and flows, everything has its polarities.

You have to experience pain in order to recognise peace, or be sans pain to experience pleasure. You have to rest in order to work, you have to sleep in order to be awake and alert. In manifesting, there are times of action and then there are times that you have to allow the path to show itself. Just like when you are up in a hot-air balloon, you genuinely cannot control your direction or steer the balloon; you just fly in the direction of the wind—so you either stop blowing gas and hot air into the envelope causing it to go up, or allow it to cool so it comes down. This can be likened to more 'doing' or more 'allowing'.

F. Scott Fitzgerald pointed out, 'The test of a first-rate intelligence is the ability to hold two opposed ideas in the mind at the same time and still retain the ability to function.'

Understand that when there is an 'up' there has to be a 'down', and then there is also a 'mid-air'. We all possess feminine and masculine attributes—estrogen and testosterone— and both are needed in order to survive. Similarly, *doing* and *allowing* are both parts of your growth. 'Giving' and 'Receiving' are both parts of your journey to manifesting.

Pain vs Pleasure

Think of a time in your life when you felt excruciating pain in your body due to an illness or a fall. I have had a few encounters with physical pain. There was natural childbirth over 2 decades ago, but that was not too unbearable for me; the pain that strongly comes to mind are my sore-throats. Growing up, I used to get a sore throat quite often and finally in my early 20s it was occurring almost once a month. They were unendurable, and I am saying this knowing that I have a pretty high pain-threshold. After seeing a few Otorhinolaryngologists or in simpler terms Ear, Nose and Throat specialists, the prognosis was inevitable surgery, to remove my tonsils. The night before my scheduled surgery was to take place in Singapore, my friends decided to take me out for a few drinks. The few drinks turned into a few *more* drinks. To help the hangover, I was advised to take an 'Alka Seltzer' which, by the way, contains Aspirin. So, on the morning of surgery I told my surgeon that I had a reaction to aspirin (since I was allergic to it) and that I was still in my hangover but he did not agree to my repeated requests for postponing the surgery. His decision led to extreme disappointment. Anyway, I was wheeled in to the theatre and back, then I still had a phobia of needles, so when the anaesthesiologist came in with his foot-long syringe, I almost passed out, almost making his job redundant.

All this was after having my daughter, so I had already dealt with childbirth, yet this was extremely scary for me. Before they knocked me out, I remember asking if going through this surgery will ensure I will never have a painful sore throat. What I distinctly also remember is the reply the surgeon gave in his thick Singaporean accent, 'Malti, *ah*, we are just removing your tonsils, not your entire throat, so you will still have sore-throats *lah*.'

'What? Then why do I even want to go through with this surgery?' came a fading thought. But before I could protest and run away, the anaesthesia had taken effect and I was unconscious and all I remember is waking up to the disgusting taste in my mouth followed by the growing, searing pain in my throat and in my ears. The morphine wore off in a few hours and because of my drug allergies, there was not much they could give me for the pain once I was discharged from hospital.

The post-surgery agony was more painful than any of the sore throats I had ever experienced and I remember making deals with God, to please swap this pain for anything else in the world. *Please take my throat!* I am telling this story to explain how I was willing to give up almost anything, even sell my soul, to be pain free. Nothing else mattered, my relationships, finances, weight, all I wanted was to be pain-free. This taught me a huge lesson in polarities. I wasn't even trying for pleasure, the absence of pain was all I wanted.

Can you think of a time when all you wanted was to be pain-free? The morning I woke up to being pain-free I was so so happy and grateful but then it was soon forgotten, because the natural state for most of us is to be relatively pain-free and we forget to be grateful for it. It is only when in pain that we become aware of being 'pain-free'. Yes there were mornings of less pain, but it was still painful and there was not much else I could think about, so that constant focus on the pain obviously made it worse. Despite soothing salt water gargles or anesthetic mouthwashes, only time took care of it. I had to bear the pain and allow time to heal me.

Think of a time when you felt excruciating emotional anguish, the loss of a loved one, a breakup, or a betrayal.

Yes I have a story here again, which I will share later. I experienced a break-up and it was a stabbing pain. Then, too, all I wanted was to be pain-free and the hardest thing in the world was to not think of the pain; as much as I knew, I could not stop not thinking of the blue ball. I kept telling myself not to think about it. Again, I had to allow time to do its work. And it did. One morning, I woke up to literally feeling pain-free. The ache and the hole in my heart and the hollow in my stomach were gone. Then came the stage of getting used to the absence of the pain, which had also become a habit. My hands would clench in my sleep and I noticed my face often screwing up to look like someone holding anguish. It took time and it did go away, it was replaced with joy. So from pain to pain-free to pleasure. I actually noticed myself looking for the pain and found that it was not there anymore.

It is only when we can connect with our feelings of pain and hurt that we can feel love again. It is only when you have experienced pain that you can be grateful for being pain-free and then enjoy pleasure. We have nerve sensors for our feelings. The same nerve that allows pain in is the valve that allows us to experience pleasure.

As the Australian musician Delta Goodrem so aptly sang in her song *Bare Hands*,

A little pain lets you know you're alive
We gotta live and love, not just survive

Then there was a car accident I mentioned, where I severely injured my coccyx, the base of my spine. Again it was excruciating and I could not sit. I could walk, even dance but I could not sit on it. That one never went away completely, but now I only feel it if I invite it, like sitting in a rickshaw on an Indian road full of potholes is a good way to feel that it is still there. This relates similarly to things which are still painful but only when we aggravate it. And this can be a great analogy for how our thoughts and focus determine our experience. Why would you deliberately want to feel pain when you have a choice?

Doing vs Allowing

We want everything instantly, we want our desires to manifest immediately, now! We want fame, success, wealth and relationships—instantly. Everything in nature takes time to 'happen'. Practice patience and learn to wait. Do what you can to start the process—plant the seed in the ground, or bait the fishing line and then wait for all the elements to come into place.

You will then be guided by the Universe to take effective and inspired action for the next steps, to make a decision and propel your course. Many people get impatient and start to change things right away, not allowing the forces of nature to act and carry out the process. When you do this and react to situations, looking for the next quick solution, when you get desperate and restless, you work against nature and crush the seedlings that had already started to sprout under the visible surface of the soil.

Learning to wait in peace is a powerful attribute. There are some things that just can't happen now, no matter how hard you want them to. It is actually a relief to know that you have no power over it. It frees your energy to do other things. Picture yourself in the office where there are two people struggling to finish their work for the day. While one of them is completely at it and doing it all alone, she won't ask for help as she is a perfectionist and believes that only she can do her work perfectly, the other one stops, looks up at you and says, 'I've done the best I can, now can you please help me?' Which one will you help? When you overdo, you do not allow time or the Universe to do their part. You have taken complete ownership of the project and have completely separated yourself from all the other forces involved. Have you heard of artists, authors and musicians who tell of how the piece wrote itself? They allowed, letting an energy higher than their own to take the reins, they gave up control and perfection and just allowed the music, painting or book to flow. One definition of patience is 'doing something else in the meantime'. So, what can you do in the meantime?

Bring to mind the 'Jigsaw Puzzle Visualisation Exercise', I introduced in the earlier chapter and how the pieces are falling slowly into place. *Keep in mind that joy is not in the finishing of an activity but in doing it.* I was babysitting my dear friend's two-year-old son and we were playing with a huge animal kingdom puzzle. I was thrilled when I put the last piece in, a sense of completion and achievement, but the little one was disappointed and went on to pull them all apart again. The fun was the experience and journey of putting it together. Same with your desires.

Look with gratitude and positivity at every experience and at exactly where you are today, who you met last week and what you are doing now. You may be able to see that everything is falling into place just like the pieces of a jigsaw that were thrown up in the air, only to fall back down where they are meant to land.

Most of us have grown up believing that we have to engage ourselves in some work. And if we sit down and wait, then we are either being lazy or we are not motivated or trying hard enough. Though part of this is true—yes, you do have to get into action to get the ball rolling—but then there is a stage of having to let go and just allow. Allow other people to respond, allow time to do its part and allow yourself to learn and grow.

Congruency and parts integration – Left or Right

Coming back to the polarities, do you sometimes find yourself saying, *a part of me wants this and a part of me wants that*? I want to be successful, but I am too tired to work all day, I want to be thin but I want to eat chocolate cakes every night, I want to be in a loving relationship but I don't want to stop dating every man or woman I can or I don't want to share my space and time with another. How often have you noticed yourself saying, 'A part of me wants to be rich and successful but another part of me believes that money is the root to all evil?'

We often have conflicting parts and the best way to ensure that we don't get anywhere near our desires is to stay in this state of conflict. Think about it as trying to walk when one foot is pointing west and the other east, you are not going to go anywhere. This is the feeling of being stuck. Or think of driving when one of the tyres is skewed. In order to get anywhere we need to have all parts congruent, just like getting a wheel alignment done on your car.

There is an NLP technique that I use with my clients to help integrate these conflicting parts. If you could 'speak' to each part separately, what would their highest intention for you be? Let's take the one part that wants to eat chocolate cakes. Let's say we ask 'her' to stand on your left palm—while you have both your palms facing upwards and quite close together—and get the other part to stand on your right palm, this is the part that wants to be slimmer and lighter.

If we ask the left part why she wants the cake, she may say it is delicious, to feel good, to enjoy the taste, and if we keep prodding and asking 'why?' again and again, attempting to get to the highest intention of that part, we may come up with an answer like 'to be happy'.

Now if you put the part on the right side through the same line of questioning ('Why do you want to be slim?'), the answers might be to fit into my clothes, to look good, to be lighter, to look sexy, to be more attractive to men, and ultimately this side will more than likely come to the same highest want, 'to be happy'. This is when I would encourage you to bring both palms together and place them on your heart. This 'revelation' often makes us feel quite humbled and peaceful and we can practice this any time we identify conflicting parts that come in the way of us manifesting our desires. It is rather rare that one of the desires you have in your mind, while reading this book, is something as trivial as eating chocolate cakes every day. So in the hierarchy of desires, eating the cake falls way below the desire to be slim although both parts only want you to be happy. So once you can integrate the parts, the 'bigger' desire for now will become more dominant and therefore better guide you in making your choices.

Same goes for the man who wants to be in a relationship and yet also wants to be free to keep all his space and his time to himself. Or the person who wants to make a success of their business but also wants to play video games all day. Or the person who wants to stay in their job but also wants to turn their passion or talent into a business.

Identify the highest want for both parts and then it will become easy for you to decide what to do next. Find congruency between *what you say* and *what you do*. As they say, as powerful as words are, actions can sometimes speak louder still.

Saying No to say Yes

We meet countless people every week, some are attracted to us in some way or the other and I don't just mean romantically, but even for work, or to become friends. We don't have to say 'yes' to that all the time. *We can choose.* Romantically, if we meet someone who does not fit in with the kind of person we want to be with, we absolutely can say 'no'. If we decide to give them a chance and entertain their advances in the start and then realise that they don't treat us the way we want to be treated in a relationship, we can say 'no'. Men and women like to say 'I always attract the wrong guy/girl' when that is not true. The truth is, you attract people and then you choose to accept, allow them to hang around and treat you the exact way you don't want to be treated. So, don't blame the law of attraction for your choice to accept.

Have you ever been Ballroom dancing, where the women wait, while they pretend they are not waiting, for a man to walk up to them holding his hand out in a gesture and saying 'May I...have this dance?' If the woman says 'Yes', she is saying 'No' to all the other possible people she could dance with instead, at least for the duration of one song. If she does not like the way this particular man looks, smells, speaks or dances, then saying 'Yes', just for the sake of it, 'accepting' his offer would be silly. She is passing up on the opportunity to be asked by someone dynamic and dashing that she may truly want to dance with. You are not attracting the wrong people, you are simply accepting them. Saying 'No' frees you up so you can say 'Yes' when you truly want to.

You have to learn to be discerning of all your choices. Remember when you say 'yes' to something you are saying 'no' to something else and vice versa. In fact you sometimes have to say 'No' to one thing in order to say 'Yes' to the one you truly want to say yes to. When you say 'No' to chocolate cake enough times, you are saying 'Yes' to being slim.

In between yes and no is the negotiation to revert at a later time, this is when you say, 'I will let you know'. Even if you are saying it to yourself. Think of an invitation as an opportunity to act. When you are unsure about what to do, you can defer your response by saying 'I will let you know if I will be able to make it in a few days', then you wait. Wait for signs and for inspiration. If, then, you hear that all your friends are going, or if the host calls you up three times and insists you come, or if you find out that it is at the place that you have been dying to go to anyway, then I would look at that as a sign to go.

This is the case with all your 'invitations' to act. When in doubt, wait, if you need to, negotiate and then commit to the time frame you want to respond by and then wait for the signs. As harsh as this may sound, I believe that when you say 'Yes' to something you don't want to do, it can be likened to agreeing to being raped. What are you not saying 'No' to in your life? They say when the lord closes a window, he opens a door. I think that when you are already thinking of saying no, you are closing the slightly ajar window and allowing the doors of possibility to fly open.

What are you going to say 'No' to, today? What will you be saying 'Yes' to when you do this?

Clean up to make space for new to come in

Imagine again that you are driving around in a convertible and that the sky is raining down with cash and all the other things you desire in life, wonderful people, great opportunities, uplifting thoughts and all the goodness you want.

Now imagine you are driving with the top closed. Not desired! Because all the good things that are raining from the skies will now only fall into all the other open-topped convertibles driving down this road of manifesting desires.

That was the easy part, flick the switch and open the top. Now, if you can, imagine that you have all the seats and space in your car full with the people and stuff in your life. The good stuff raining from the skies will still have nowhere to fall into your car, so how do you clear the space?

Imagine that all the independent and positive people in your life have their own open-topped convertibles and are driving down the highway with you, alongside. So now you know that the people you are carrying around with you are just taking up space that is preventing your good stuff from falling in.

Think of all your contacts on your phone, all the invitations that you receive that distract you from your goal, the exes, the women or men that you have no desire to pursue a relationship with, and their being around in your head space is keeping you from meeting the people who you potentially may want to meet, the business opportunities that sadly have not gone anywhere and don't feel so inspiring anymore. Things on your to-do list that you know you are never going to do. Clothes or jewellery that you will never wear, books you will never read. Discard, exchange, sell or give them away.

Think of all the clutter in your drawers, cupboards, on your desktop and in your email box as taking up space in this convertible of yours. Think of the unfinished things you want to do and the tasks you have floating around in your head as also taking up more space, be it in the glove compartment or under the seats, they are taking up cubic space in your car. If you believed this, who and what would you want to eliminate as soon as possible?

Firstly, clean up your physical space, then clear up your computer space, these are the easy tasks. There are only 3 steps involved in cleaning out any 'space'.

Step 1 – Stock-take:

Take everything out and put them where you can see them. If they are thoughts sitting in your head, you need to write them all down.

Step 2 – Sort into 3 categories:
1. Love
2. Delete
3. Keep For Later

Once you have sorted them, relook each pile, find a neat place for the love ones, delete or throw out all those you don't like or need anymore, and with the Keep For Later pile, set a date by which you will want to look at it again.

With the people that you don't want in your life, it could be because being around them or hearing from them does not give you any joy. If you can, delete them from your phone, email lists, social media. Look out for constant drama, or conversations that drag you into a realm of complaining and criticising. You could tell them that you are working on a project and need to be left alone for a while. If they can respect that, then perhaps you may be able to reconsider your decision to delete them and instead have them in your 'outer-circle' for now.

Be strong about setting up your boundaries. Remember, say 'no' to say 'yes' to something more important to you. Don't worry about what they may think of you. This is different for family, for whom you have an underlying love and concern, in which case be discerning enough to put them in the 'Love' pile and work on your boundaries and communicating style with them.

Work on all areas of cleaning up within the same time frame.

Just making the list—even if you do not throw out or delete the things and people that don't make you feel more connected to your purpose, your desires and your source energy—just that act of putting them in a list will help send out invisible 'DND', 'Do not Disturb' signals to them if they are sensitive. But if they continue to seep into your life, then more drastic measures may be needed, in the form of a conversation to actually stop communicating with them and deleting their contact from your phone and social media profile.

Hearing No

Do you hold back from getting close with people because of the fear of rejection? Remember when you do that, you are causing yourself to miss out on the potential happiness, love, fun and excitement that relating closely with someone can bring to you. A great way to put the fear of rejection behind you is to replace it with the positive and empowering thought that 'If you never put yourself in a position where someone can say "No", then you are also closing yourself off to the opportunity of someone saying "YES."' This brings me back to Ballroom dancing. My father used to tell us stories of how, when he was in his twenties in Singapore, he learnt Cha-Cha and Rock and Roll, both needed that he practiced with a lady-partner and so, once a week, he would go out to test-drive his new skills and he had to approach women and ask them to dance. This meant that he had to be willing to accept "No" sometimes. Well, dad was a very handsome man (still is) so he didn't have to hear 'No' much.

In an Anthony Robbins seminar I attended, I heard the story of Colonel Sanders of Kentucky Fried Chicken (KFC). How many times do you think Colonel Sanders heard 'No' before getting the answer he wanted? He was refused 1,009 times before he heard his first 'Yes'. Whenever you want to submit something, sell something, count the number of attempts even if they are met with 'Nos'. The more 'Nos' you get the closer you are to the 'Yes' using Thomas Edison's strategy when inventing the light bulb. He saw each failed attempt as a validation that he was getting closer.

Power of choice

You can either be in a space of complete and implicit trust or in a space of doubt. When there is an iota of doubt, there is NO TRUST. When you believe 100 per cent, there can be magic; put a drop of doubt and all is gone. You can either come from love or fear, there is no middle ground here.

Either you do something or you don't do something, there is no try. Try putting this book down; right now, as you read this line, try to put it down. So are you still reading or did you put it down? There is no try, either you did it or you didn't. *No 'Try' only 'Do'* as the famous Yoda says in *Star Wars*.

You either respect someone or you totally invalidate them, there is no halfway again. You can be telling the truth, or you are lying, again there is no halfway.

You can take things lightly or heavily—as if nothing matters or everything matters. You can complain or you can be grateful. Either you appreciate the people and situations around you, even the weather, or you are ungrateful for it. You can look at every situation as a punishment from God or as a reward from the same God. You can look at it as a problem or an opportunity to create more change. It is up to you! *You DECIDE!* You Choose. Get off the fence, choose one way or another.

What about when you feel you have no choice and you think you just have to do something? I believe there is always choice, it is just that sometimes the price is too high to even consider the other option, so we choose one. We do have choice, the option may be death by firing squad or worse, and that is why we choose life. But never forget that we are still choosing. Try to change your language. Catch yourself each time you say 'I have to...', 'I have to go to the gym', 'I have to cook', 'I have to go to work' and notice that they are all choices. Replace 'have to' with 'want to' or 'choose to', if 'want to' does not feel right.

'I want to go to work', 'I choose to go to the gym', 'I want to finish this assignment'.

What do you value most?

Answering this question will help you understand your desires, your motives and your decision-making processes. Values are the things that matter most to us. While Security, Status and Patriotism may be highly important to you Freedom, Adventure and Money may be more important to another. This is why you often have friends say to you, 'I found a better job.' Better than what? Better in pay or in status and security? Or, 'I am moving to France for a better life.' What's a better life? Better in what sense? Or, 'Why are you with her, you can find someone much better.' Better looking? From a better family? More educated? Part of what determines that which is 'better' for us or not is our values and of course, our personal desires and our past experiences.

This is why it is truly futile to ask people for advice. Plug In instead, be silent and at source. People sometimes cannot understand our decisions, for example when I left Australia after having lived there for over 15 years to move to India, all my friends from India and from Australia could not fathom my decision. This was because of a different set of values, past experiences and desires. My move to India in 2010 was guided by my top values of Freedom, Adventure and Family and I was craving a sense of Belonging, as being of Indian Origin, I had never lived in India before then.

We already have our values, they are intrinsically built into us like an internal compass, so the shortest way to discovering what they are, is by looking at our major decisions in the past. Another way of doing this is to look at a list of prescribed or common values. I have listed a few of the more common ones below for you to have a look at.

If the ones you are looking for are not there, please just add them. Also the more extensive your vocabulary is, the more specific you can get with your value list, but the aim is not to be verbose but rather to pick the top ones that truly matter to you.

Values Clarification Exercise

Look at the list of values below and pick ten that are most important to you and circle them. Once you have done this, reduce that to five and then to three. Three top values are all you need to help you navigate through your life together with your desires, your personal declaration and your intuition. I found that I was able to group many of my values under one main value, and in that way I was able to feel complete with my top three. To me Family, Friendship, Spirituality and Compassion all fell comfortably under Love. And Success, Abundance, Luxury fell under Freedom. And Adventure, Pleasure, Variety fell under Fun. Once you have your list of 10, 5 and 3, keep them safely. You will be able to see how your life has always already been guided by these values. Choosing three does not mean that the others are not important; however, having three top values will make it so much easier for you to navigate.

List of Values	
Accomplishment	Love
Accountability	Loyalty
Adventure	Money
Beauty	Openness
Challenges	Patriotism
Charity	Peace
Cleanliness	Perfection
Commitment	Personal Growth
Communication	Perseverance
Community	Pleasure
Competence	Power
Competition	Practicality
Compassion	Preservation
Connection	Privacy
Cooperation	Progress
Coordination	Prosperity
Creativity	Punctuality
Determination	Regularity
Democracy	Reliability
Discipline	Religion

Enjoyment	Romance
Equality	Safety
Excellence	Security
Fairness	Sensitivity
Faith	Simplicity
Faithfulness	Stability
Family	Status
Freedom	Strength
Friendship	Success
Fun	Timeliness
Flirtation	Tolerance
Generosity	Tradition
Gentleness	Tranquility
Global view	Trust
Gratitude	Truth
Hard work	Unity
Happiness	Variety
Harmony	Well-being
Health	Wisdom
Honor	Innovation
Improvement	Integrity
Independence	Intelligence
Individuality	Intensity
Inner peace	Justice
Integrity	Kindness
Knowledge	Leadership

7

Letting Go

All the art of living lies in a fine mingling of letting go and holding on.
— Henry Ellis

So, what does letting go of regrets have to do with attracting positive people and positive situations in your life?

We have read that you can only expect positive outcomes when you have implicit faith. We have also read that in order to have positive outcomes and faith, we have to trust we have the capacity to choose the best option available to us at any juncture and to be open to the coincidences and signs that we experience.

To illustrate this, let's picture a game show. Look at the circumstance you are currently in as the result of picking one of four given options. Instinct is just all the collated knowledge you have gathered through your experiences, reading, listening and growing. So when you make a choice, a decision based partly on instinct and partly on the facts presented to you alerts you to understand you are choosing the best option. You may, just like in a game show, through the process of elimination know which options *not* to choose. You can also use the 'call a friend' lifeline and then you make your choice.

When we regret, we are negating all that. All the years of experience, knowledge, reading, listening, growing which amounted to who you are at the point of 'locking it in' that helped in making that choice.

To regret doing something is to believe that you chose wrongly. To dwell in regret will reinforce that you can choose wrongly again since you have done it before. This is the most fundamental reason you have to be willing to let go and move on. Regrets are just the brain's way of exploring the alternative. Remember books that have alternate endings, depending on the choices made at some pivotal moments?

Why let go and move on?

First, what is your alternative? Let us see

If you think of yourself as a magnet, out to attract all the goodness, and you are covered in these layers and specks of dust, bubbles and muck—it will surely insulate you from the 'attracting' surfaces. Apart from that, if not checked, we can let the weight of this regret immobilise or incapacitate us.

Thinking Pink Letting Go Exercise

List 12 things you regret doing or not doing and put each of these 12 things through this line of questioning.

\# Was it big or small? If it was small, drop it.

\# Is it something I did not do, that I could still do if I really want to? If yes, put it down for something you can do in future. Set a goal, a date in the future that you intend to take it on.

\# Did I hurt someone else in this process? Write the word 'forgive' next to it and we will come back to forgiveness later.

\# Am I suffering today as a result of this regret? If you answer no, scratch it off, if yes, write 'lesson to be learned' next to it.

Once you have this list, you can work through it in order to come out on the other side, having let go and ready to move on.

What are these typical regrets that are preventing good from being attracted to you? I would put them in two categories. The ones we regret doing and the ones we regret not doing. With the ones we didn't do, let's face it, if those were that important to us, we would have done it, or we knew back then that it was something we could always do. Learning to swim or ride a horse at a later stage in life, learning a new language, travelling to a particular place, inviting someone to a party would constitute the list of regrets under this category.

Even educational pursuits not endeavoured upon always have a time in the future. And we have to remember we did choose something else in its place. Romances not pursued—well, if we wanted them that badly, we would have pursued them.

The one that got away—why did he or she get away? Were we downright ready for that relationship? Did we feel undeserving of them?

What is essential is to start making decisions based on our desires. What do we really want? Once we align our decisions with what we really want, as opposed to what we feel from time to time, we will have lesser and lesser regrets.

Make a commitment to the highest desire and make all your decisions based on creating that in your life.

Our emotions are like the weather, they can be hot some days and cold on others, in fact they change from moment to moment. If we make our decisions based on how we are feeling at that point, we will choose 'wrongly'. When we have compelling desires, it makes it almost automatic to choose the way that will lead to that destination.

When unsure, sometimes the best thing to do is to do nothing. Inaction in itself is also 'doing something'. It is still choosing. When we say 'Yes' to something we are always saying 'No' to something else. So in that way, we never 'don't do' anything. We are just doing something else.

We all have memories swept under the proverbial rug that we are not proud of. Choices we made and things we pursued that did not have a desired outcome and also opportunities we missed out on because we were too afraid.

If you look at it closely, even when you have taken wrong turns, even the wrong turns have led you to interesting places.

If you could change the past, it would possibly erase some of your most memorable experiences.

Without being blasé as we can be in hindsight, there are some events and choices you still wish you didn't choose, since they may have left emotional scars. Did your choices put you and the people you care about through some tough times? This is where you have to forgive yourself. Take the time to look for loving support from the people in your life to help you put things in perspective, in order to let go and move on.

Life and death are not for us to decide no matter what the circumstances, and if, unfortunately, your negligence led to a terrible loss, your pain would have taught you enough and will save you from ever repeating the parts that you had some control over. The rest of it has to be forgiven.

Financial decisions that turned out unfavourably

Stock you bought or sold prematurely. Property you should have bought or sold. An investment you could have made.

There is a distinction between a missed opportunity and regret.

When you start with a compelling desire in mind, you will see opportunities more clearly, hear the knock more frequently and respond more daringly.

Haven't you experienced wanting to buy a particular make of a car and then noticed you started seeing them all over the place, like I did with my convertible? Were more of them created just for you to look at or were they always there but you are only noticing them now?

What you focus on, is what you have. If you are unsure about what your focus has been over the last three months, look at what you have.

A few months ago I set out on this journey and today, when I look around me, based on these results, my focus over the last few months is evident. Every seed I planted has started to sprout into seedlings and they all derive their nutrients from the same root, my compelling desire.

My choices were guided by these desires. When opportunities knocked I opened the door, sometimes the window, or at least looked through the peephole. Everything that was in alignment with what I declared I wanted started to scream out to me and I made my choices. Every single moment of every single day, making decisions around my compelling desires.

That is how we manifest and attract what and who we want in our lives.

So if your regret has been a lost financial opportunity, get clear again on what you *really* want, your compelling desire, so that the next opportunity that comes your way won't be missed. Trust yourself—the knowledge that your experiences have given you—and choose.

If you have put your child through difficult times based on the choices you made, then forgive yourself. By trusting that as a parent it was intrinsic that whatever you chose, whatever you did, though the outcome hurt your child, your intention was the opposite. But based on what you knew and the resources available to you back then, you made a choice yet the outcome was unfavorable. See the lesson, forgive yourself, seek forgiveness from them and let it go. If you trust that everything is perfect, as harsh and unbelievable as this may sound right now, perhaps that was a necessary lesson that your child learnt that would help them prevent hurting themselves in the future. Perhaps, in them seeing some of your own relationship and financial mis-haps, you have unwittingly paved a new path for your child.

Letting go feels like this
Scrunch up your shoulders to your ears, frown your hardest frown, tense all your muscles as you inhale...hold it there for sometime and then exhale, making the sound 'Ahhhhh' letting it all go, dropping the shoulders and smiling at the end.

Let it go!

Lessons learnt
Who knows what the knowledge and learning from those unfavourable experiences have saved us from? Experiences we chose and the ones that *happened* to us all possibly took us down a path that actually saved us from a fate worse

than that. Trust that every night when you go to sleep, all the knowledge you picked up from your experiences stay with you, even though the actual experience is finished and over. Trust that one day, when posed with a question or a dilemma, you will instinctively make your decision based on all the knowledge, hindsight and wisdom you picked up from all your past experiences.

Think about a small car accident when no one gets hurt and the impact is taken mostly by the car. We feel regret at the inconvenience and expenditure, but what if the driving lesson we learnt from that small accident is the skill we needed to learn that would keep us alive on the roads?

What would we change if we had to do it all over again? Regret can be useful in the short term when we learn immediate lessons and commit not to repeat them. But in the long term, regret has an insidious edge to it. When we start second-guessing our past, it is a short step to second-guessing our present and ultimately ourselves. If the things that brought us to where we are today were mistakes, then that would imply where we are today and who we are today is a mistake. It is far more empowering to believe where we are today is perfect and where we need to be for our highest good and the greater good of all concerned.

In order to move forward we have to be willing to let go of the past.

Forgive yourself, forgive the other
He that cannot forgive others breaks the bridge over which he must pass himself; for every man has need to be forgiven

— Thomas Fuller

Forgive the part of the other person which is just a part of you wanting to be acknowledged. When we feel regret, we relive guilt, sadness or anger. Allowing yourself to experience these feelings fully with the intention of moving forward can help you stop revisiting them. The only way out is through, allow yourself a few moments to face and experience the feelings once and for all, cry, mourn, feel the pain. Seek for forgiveness from the people involved if that is possible. If, unfortunately, it is not, know the person we truly need to forgive is ourselves. Even the other person represents a part of ourselves we have not forgiven. Forgive, from a place of knowing you did indeed choose the best option available to you at the time, based on what you knew at that time. Forgiveness is not a chore, it is a gift. It has little to do with the other person. Most of us have a childhood that may need forgiveness. Forgive your parents. Reflect on those pivotal years during which your personality developed and write a letter to your father or mother (this is not to send to them, but just as an exercise). 'Dad, although I didn't agree at the time, I understand now why you….' Next, even if it feels uncomfortable, list the things that you wish they had done, done differently or not done, 'Dad, I wish you…' 'Mum, I wish you didn't…'

Often we do not have the opportunity to ask for, or give, forgiveness where it is so needed and that can lead to years of being stuck and being blocked. Recently, and in synchronicity, while I was writing this book, an old client of mine reported that he had received an unexpected call from his ex-wife apologising to him for all the pain she had caused him through her affair, back when they were married over a decade ago. Lucky for the ex-wife, my client had long ago forgiven her but she needed to apologise for herself, so that she could move on. Forgiving is 'for giving'. In order to give and receive in our future from others we have to forgive the past.

The good news is like a snowball rolling down a slope, we are learning more and more and making ourselves better equipped for future decisions. Positively, regret is the mind's way of exploring 'what-if' and so think about that. Forgiveness is possible when we understand that even if life is rewound, we would have chosen the same thing again, because based on our resources at that time, it was our only choice. When the time comes when someone truly apologises to you from the heart, forgive them, let them know that you have let it go.

Trust that we are essentially good and loving beings and would never have deliberately or unnecessarily chosen a path that caused pain or suffering to anyone, our selves included.

We have been programmed to always choose comfort over pain. Being comfortable is a level of being alive. This stems from our basic survival instinct. We will choose the painless option, always. Sometimes, though, it would be the least uncomfortable option. Like choosing to take a painful vaccination in the form of an injection instead of risk dying of tuberculosis.

This brings to mind another story...

Imagine you are in a room, out of a James Bond or Indiana Jones movie. The walls are closing in, literally. Imagine you can see the red digital countdown and you have 60 seconds.

59...58...57...42...41...39...

Time is running out!

You are alone in the room, the ceiling is high and on the ground, you see three covered manholes.

You lift the lid off the first one and it is a sewer. The stench is so strong it infuses the entire room. Just like the one little Jamal in the movie *Slumdog Millionaire* jumped into to get to the famous Hindi movie star Amitabh Bachchan when he was locked in the outdoor toilet. Yes, faeces. It stinks, but it is shallow. Disgusted, you put the lid back on.

22...21...19...

You open the next manhole and you see great white sharks and crocodiles swimming in here. Petrified, you close this manhole, too.

16...15...12...

You open the third one and in here are spiders, venomous snakes and scorpions. Now you know you are in an old Indiana Jones movie.

9...8...7...6...

Time is running out as it does in most difficult situations, we have to choose. Inaction is not an option as the walls are closing in...you can almost feel them touch you.

5...4...3...

So, what do you do? Basic survival instinct will choose life. So you take a deep breath, pinch your nose tight and jump into the first hole—the sewer.

So, now you are alive and wading in smelly shit.

Not nice at all, but you are alive. ALIVE, and *not* DEAD.

As time goes by, you swim and wade through the sewer. You are initially grateful to be alive, then you forget the other alternatives from which you had to choose and you become totally present to your current smelly predicament. People around look and point, 'Look at him swimming in that sewer', but no one knew your available options, did they? They, too, would have chosen the same.

The point is, we do choose the best option available to us at any given time. We have to trust that we do.

Swimming in murky waters in my life has given me a lot of tools. I now know that I can achieve anything I set my heart on. I also know how to recognise when my options are not desirable but sometimes one is just less undesirable.

Regret is, in a sense, what is left when you subtract what you knew *then* from what you know *now*.

Be careful though, we can sometimes be horribly conniving even with ourselves. Deceiving ourselves by using guilt and regret as a way to invalidate our 'wrong doings' to make us good people again. We feel good about ourselves again because we 'feel bad' about the bad we did.

Forgiveness is for you, not for them

It is a way of releasing yourself from the need for the person you feel hurt by to do anything to make you feel better.

And there's no requirement that you forget, but simply forgive, let go of holding on to the pain and holding the other person responsible for your happiness. See them as having done the best they could, even if it was the worst for you. It was still the best they could do. And let go.

Yet, we do it all the time. We linger in the past, thinking of the 'what ifs' and the 'if onlys'. Agonising over the 'could haves' and 'should haves'. What is done is done. It cannot be otherwise. It cannot be changed. We are here now in this present moment and that is all we have.

Don't berate yourself for what you could have done better or how you could have been more understanding. You have probably been terribly hurt but have also learnt a few valuable lessons about life and love in the process.

How to let go of lost love

If you believe yourself unfortunate, because you have 'loved and lost', perish the thought. One who has loved truly, can never lose entirely.

There should be no disappointment over love. No experience, which touches the human heart with a spiritual force, can possibly be harmful, except through ignorance or jealousy.

Memories of love never pass. They linger, guide and influence long after the source of stimulation has faded. There is nothing new in this. Every person, who has been moved by GENUINE LOVE, knows that it leaves enduring traces upon the human heart. The effect of love endures, because love is spiritual in nature.

–Excerpt from *Think and Grow Rich*–by Napolean Hill– written in 1937, that is almost 75 years ago. (Quoted here with consent from The Napolean Hill Foundation. www.naphill.org)

Was this the one that felt as if it was meant to be? You felt like the entire Universe conspired to bring the two of you together, against all odds, and all the signs were positive and pointed in the direction of the two of you being together? How do you let go of a relationship like this? I have been there, against my judgments and all warning bells going off, I only looked for the signs that pointed towards *this one person instead of taking heed of the warnings to stay away.*

Losing a loved one through a break-up emulates the same sense of loss and grief as losing someone to death. Some of us may breeze through the five stages of grief, because in some way, we already went through them whilst still in the relationship. In my case, I sobbed for months before the actual break-up because I knew it was gone way before I formalised it.

Your hopes in the future died when this relationship ended, the vision of what your life was going to look like is shattered and you have no idea what to replace that image with. It is a cycle and many people do end up stuck in the anger, this can be awfully sad and self-destructive.

The five stages of grief:

\# Denial – 'this can't be happening', or 'I don't believe this!'

\# Anger – 'why me?', blaming the other person and projecting all other hurt and anger on this person.

\# Bargaining – this often takes place before the loss. Attempting to make deals with the partner who is leaving, or attempting to make deals with God to stop or change the loss. Begging, wishing, praying for them to come back.

\# Depression – overwhelming feelings of hopelessness, frustration, bitterness, self-pity, mourning the loss of the person as well as the hopes, dreams and plans for the future.

\# Acceptance – you have to accept the loss, not just try to bear it quietly. Realise that it takes two to make or break a relationship. Our goals turn toward personal growth. Stay with fond memories of the person and we let go and forgive.

Be very honest now

How long were you in the relationship?

How many days were you angry and felt you would be better off alone, or wondered if you could change her or him?

How often were you drunk when you felt totally happy with each other?

How many hours in a day were you truly satisfied and happy?

How much time did you say or think 'this will get better'?

How intimate were you, honestly, towards the end of the relationship?

Physically? Emotionally?

How well did you communicate? How much did you openly say and how much did you hold back?

How many times did you outwardly or inwardly complain about your partner?

Be truthful, look at the facts and ask yourself: what advice would you give to your closest friend, your brother or sister, or your children if you witnessed them go through this relationship? Often, we are less myopic when looking at the people we care about most and we see things clearly but when we are involved ourselves, our vision is grossly distorted.

This is where you have to be completely positive and have utter faith in the Universe—that the two of you were brought together to go through the learning and the evolution that you can only do in a relationship. As you may already know, it is in a relationship more than anywhere else that we can uncover who we are.

So look at the relationship as a course or a workshop, where you got to learn certain things about yourself and now know that the unique learning is embedded in you. The next person in your life in an intimate relationship will be attracted to the 'you post the ex'!

Let them go truly. If you hear that they have moved on and are in a new relationship, wish them well in your heart. If you have ever sold a home, or a car, because you have outgrown it, does it mean that the house or car should remain unused in a museum? Do you want to be the eternal curator?

You can't stop thinking of your ex. You have to find other things to think about or focus on. Remember, whatever you do, do NOT think of a BLUE ball now.

As you heal, explore answers to questions such as, 'Who am I now?' Take time to get to know yourself. One mistake many people make after a relationship ends is almost immediately try to find a new partner.

During this time, focus on healing…on learning and growing and on getting to know yourself again. Know that we are not the same person yesterday that we are today. We are all transient and who we are at any given moment is changing. We are not the person we are when we step into a movie hall or read a new book, we all come out slightly altered, knowing and realising something we did not know before.

Many of us change when in a relationship, we try to mould ourselves to better fit in or accommodate the other person…we are a part of two and often put our own preferences on the back burner to either enjoy the other person's ways or just to spend more time together. This is the time to be YOU again and get to know the YOU that you have evolved into 'post your ex'. Make choices about every little thing independently, like what to eat, listen to, where to go and what to wear. And even if you notice that some of these choices are influenced by your ex—these are things you adopted because you liked them and it is not a bad thing to inculcate them. If being with them encouraged you to replace some disempowering habits, like for example overeating, smoking or drinking too much, then instead of being childlike and restarting just because the relationship is over, keep the new habits and discard the old ones for good and for yourself. Be grateful that this relationship helped you to change that.

Honour the love
Do something to honour and cherish the true connection between your ex and you. There was a wonderful part of him or her, a loving and nurturing part. There was love for you; there may still be love for you. You may always love that part of your ex or you may not, it does not matter. What matters is that you honour them. Not being willing to do that is invalidating a time in your life and discrediting yourself for your choices back then.

When you are ready, send thoughts of peace, healing and joy to your ex whenever thoughts of your past relationship cross your mind. Whenever you miss him or her, send him or her your love, while keeping your distance and protecting yourself from his or her hurtful behaviour. This is forgiving and letting go. By honouring the good of the relationship, you become free of the anger you feel towards him or her. By honouring the gifts he or she gave you, instead of focusing on what he or she did not give you, you will begin to feel peace and gratitude for all that you shared together. This is how you embrace yourself, your decisions and your implicit faith in the Universe.

Remember that this is not 'Project getting over your ex', or 'Project dealing with the breakup'. Relationships and romantic love are usually started because of our hormones, attraction and chemical changes in our brain...but break-ups are usually based on a rational decision and it is painful because sometimes the rational decision is made by only one of you first, leaving the other one feeling dumped and rejected. For both of you though, man or woman, the one who ended it first or not, this is 'Project living your best life now'.

How to move on?

When you find yourself thinking of the regret, turn your thoughts to the things you have learnt and the opportunities now yours—even if they are not what you would have preferred. There is a lesson even in pain and sadness. Look for the lesson and focus on it instead of what might have been.

As my daughter Drishti very wisely pointed out to me, *'The lessons we have to learn in life are destined, but the methods in which we learn these lessons are dependent on our choices. Someone who has control issues with their father and has not dealt with them growing up, will inadvertently recreate them later on in other relationships.'* Someone who can't distinguish between assertiveness and aggression will also recreate instances to practice and learn.

Look at what you do have and all that you have already created in your life. Do a once-over. Sometimes all we need to do when we are feeling most lost and forlorn is to do a check of our present to be able to let go of the past and of our self-professed mistakes.

Somewhat like when you are about to travel, you'll quickly do a once-over to ensure you have your

Wallet;

Passport;

Cash;

Amex.

and then you let out a sigh of relief and feel a sense of I've got it all!

I am ready, bring it on!

In life, once in a while, especially when you are feeling overwhelmed or restless, it is important to do that is 'Once-over'.

Health – check!

Health and safety of close immediate family that truly matter – check!

Roof – check!

Laughter – check!

Hot water – check!

Food – check!

Then you can say to yourself, I have everything I need today, I am ready for life, bring it on! Feel that sense of peace. That everything is OK, everything is in fact perfect, exactly as it should be—right now!

Don't re-live the event over and over by continually telling others what happened. You could actually become 'addicted' to the sympathy! You will also be sending off that energy and, in turn, attracting the similar experience again and again. The law of attraction does not know to differentiate. Feel love, attract love, feel successful, attract success, feel famous and attract opportunities for more fame, feel sadness and rejection and attract more rejection. What you give out will perpetuate. Remember the Remixes we got into in Chapter 5, rewrite the story of this event, whether it was a love or a venture, whatever it was, rewrite it and do the exercise on finding what was great about them.

In hindsight, we do always choose the best possible option, just like the swimming in the sewer example, so regret in most instances is an absolute waste of energy. Acknowledge yourself for your greatness and your instincts and know that you always do your best even when the outcomes don't appear that way.

Thinking Pink Letting Go Exercise

\# Ask for forgiveness from the one you still feel you need it from. 'Please forgive me, I am so sorry.' If they are available. If they are not, then forgive yourself and express your forgiveness of yourself to someone who will listen.

\# If you feel you still need to forgive someone, then truly forgive them and let it go. 'I forgive you truly.' Make contact if you can and even if they are not available to you, write your forgiveness and send it to them. Let it go. If they are no more, then honour them with a small ritual letting them know that you have truly forgiven them for the pain and have let the pain go.

\# If you can think of something, someone or a habit that does not serve you anymore, let it go.

8

Coincidences and Intuition

Coincidences are spiritual puns.
— G.K. Chesterton

You can think that everything you experience is sheer coincidence or logical evolution, or you can believe that it is synchronicity, equivalent to magic. I am sure you have experienced it many a time; like when you are thinking of someone and they call you, when you open the newspaper and find exactly what you were speaking about the day before, or when you turn on the radio or TV and your favourite song is playing.

Or is it, as Carl Jung coined the term, synchronicity, what he called the 'acausal connecting principle' that links mind and matter. He said this underlying connectedness manifests itself through meaningful coincidences that cannot be explained by cause and effect. Such synchronicities occur, he theorised, when a strong need arises in the psyche of an individual.

I remember driving my daughter to school one morning, with my 'feel-good' music playing and it had rained earlier but the sun was out, I was feeling happy and Plugged In and suddenly I sensed that there was a rainbow. I looked up in the sky and there it was. I love seeing rainbows and perhaps because it is a frequent phenomenon in Sydney skies, on some level, I knew that there would be a rainbow in the sky that morning. All the elements were there...so was it synchronicity, did I manifest it or was it nothing?

I was told by a friend to buy a pair of ceramic love-birds for good feng shui and keep them on my bedside to attract a romantic relationship. I haven't found a pair yet, though lately, every morning when I go to turn my kettle on and I look out the kitchen window, I see love birds and I watch them going through their dance of intimacy. The female bows and the male pecks at her feathers just around her neck and then he bows and she does the same with her beak. It is so sweet to watch this and I see it every day now. Coincidence? Logical?

A sceptic would possibly call all this a post hoc fallacy. This is when people doubt the powers of manifesting, their personal power and want to question the unseen energies.

What would it mean to you if you can use your intuition and you are always accurate and guided? Even the wrong turns are the right ones, symbolically and physically. Every path introduces you to different experiences, lessons and people. Using your powers of intuition and synchronicity is just learning to read the sign-posts better, to notice the guidance that is coming from inside. Everything is perfect!

When I was not sure about a possible path to take, a business opportunity, a potential company or person to collaborate with, I went with my gut and I always saw numerous signs that led me towards following the path and going with the flow. The signs showed up everywhere—bumping into people randomly at airports who passed statements that affirmed that I was headed where I needed to go—they were like guiding angels to show me that the path I was on was the one which was meant to be.

The specific person I needed to get in touch with happened to be staying at the same hotel I was in? The book I wanted to reference almost fell on my head, off the bookshelf? Have you ever had experiences like this? A client of mine was sitting in his office watching a DVD of an artist he most admired and the very next da, that artist walked into his office.

My brother and I were the presenters at a family wedding and we wanted to have more time on stage, but were not allowed to due to tight schedules but, as it were, a mis-hap occurred at the function, forcing us to take the stage and have more time on the floor.

I found a *mala* (holy beads) that had been hanging on my bedpost with a label on it. It was given to me a year ago, but I hadn't touched it. I picked it up a few days ago and found that the label was pertinent to my life now. It said 'Om Namah Shiva' and just as I had re-started my journey in writing this book, all signs led me to that particular mantra. I even listened to a beautifully soothing version of it on my iTunes on repeat as I finished this book.

My dates in transit in Singapore coincided with a reunion with an old friend coming from San Francisco, who I went to school with 25 years ago, then on my last day—again in transit in Singapore—I had gone to my bank locker in the most obscure area and I bumped into my best friend Kiran who I was trying to call, while she was trying to call me.

There was significance at every step. Colours, music, lyrics...all in synch with what I was thinking and feeling in the moment. As if the whole world was my personal movie and every detail had been choreographed perfectly to appeal to my senses.

So what was different? *I had decided what I wanted*. The decision was made on all levels of my consciousness. Conscious, subconscious and super-conscious. The congruency is what turned me into a powerful magnet for all I wanted.

I was singing a song in the gym shower and as I was walking by the chicken shop on the way back home from the gym, the same old song was playing on their system. Almost like Déjà vu in reverse. Déjà vu is a sense you get of having been in exactly the same moment before while you are experiencing it for the first time and synchronicity is when you can see the thread that connects all your experiences leading up to the one you are in now.

Notice the choreography of the course of events that needs to take place in order for you to witness these signs.

In a later chapter we will read about expressing gratitude and I shall suggest that you write in my *Gratitude Journal* every night. A by-product of doing so is that when you look back through your journal after a few months, you will find that you have important and useful databases. One, that of people and events that you were grateful for—so you can connect the dots and see the synchronicity for yourself, and two, you will have a mind bank of things and people to be grateful for.

Intuition

The only real valuable thing is intuition.
  — Albert Einstein

Have you ever felt something and said it to someone and had them react totally surprised, saying, 'who told you?' But no one had told you anything. This has happened to me on many occasions—I just knew and I was right. What you know without knowing how you know, that is intuition.

I have got a few friends into trouble, by making people think that a common friend had leaked information, which they had not! But it is sometimes easier for people to believe that they have been 'betrayed' or 'spoken-about' rather than believe that someone is just intuitive. As a life coach, and I coach only by phone, I have a small ritual before I start, where I Plug In and ask to be an instrument for my client; often on the call, I check in and trust my 'gut-instinct' to say or ask what comes to me and, almost always, it is incredibly relevant to my client. What is this magical inspiration?

Have you noticed that it is through our intuition and instincts that we stumble upon coincidences? How do we dispel this intuition?

Trust that we gather information and store it in our bank, but often it is like a bank account where you don't know the balance. But when you go to withdraw from it, the funds are there. Trust that your intuition or your gut instinct comes to you from the innumerable things you know. You may not even know you know it, but you do.

The standard definition of intuition is 'knowledge gained of something without the use of reasoning or the five basic senses'.

Many of the successful people I have spoken to share with me that they made their decisions based on their gut instinct. Honing this instinct and becoming open to receiving this invaluable channel for information is essential to manifesting. Make it a frequent practice to sit in silence for a few moments everyday, Plug In and be open to 'listening' to anything that comes up, then go about your day welcoming these signs.

Be open-minded—I use a trigger to remind me to be open-minded to another's opinion or a concept. I uncross my legs and arms, when I know I want to learn something or I think I may hear things that may be contradictory to what

I already know and believe. Being open-minded helps you to absorb more information.

Start playing with it in small ways to test your intuition. When in a room full of people, find the time and space to observe and feel who is in the room or on the Metro or bus with you.

A game I play is to pick out 3 or more people and see what my intuition says about them. I make mental notes about them and then later I try to create the opportunity to see if I was right.

Intuition is a muscle that needs to be used in order to strengthen it.

There is a bank of greater intelligence that is accessible to everyone. This intelligence exceeds far beyond our limited personal reasoning. I believe that as we go through our days we are gatherers of information received from all our senses. Because the conscious mind cannot process that much information, most of it is absorbed into our subconscious.

A few years ago, I was celebrating New Years' Eve in St Marten in the Caribbean at a huge nightclub and during the night, I visited the women's restroom there. The place was packed with people and one had to squeeze through hundreds of people just to get out. Later when I left at about 3 am, I touched my earlobe and noticed that I was missing one earring. I was wearing diamond hoops given to me by my mother. It was a valuable piece of jewellery, plus it had huge sentimental value to me. Something in me told me to go back inside the club despite the odds. I did. I retraced some of my steps, looked on the floor and under the sofas and even sent messages to some of my friends, who were still in there, to look out for it. It was dark and crowded but I was determined. I finally retraced my steps back to the same restroom and there it was on the vanity next to the sinks, hours later. Coincidence or good luck or did I know? What is knowing?

Our conscious mind is extremely selective of what it filters in. In NLP we refer to this selection as the information filtering process. This includes Deleting, Distortion and Generalisation. What gets through the filters is what we call 'knowing'.

Filtering through deletion

We delete when we omit and do not even notice some information coming to us through our senses. We focus only on the ones we want to. A classic example of this is when you observe silence for a few moments and get your self to truly listen to the sounds in your space, suddenly some outside sounds become apparent, the cars, birds, even the hum of a fan or air-conditioner, which earlier were not even there. This is a self and sanity preservation filter, if we did not omit or delete what our senses are receiving then we would not be able to focus on anything.

Filtering through distortion

Distortions are a way of filtering our sensory information so that it fits with what we expect or believe. We are making misinterpretations of reality. When you have a misunderstanding, which you later clear with a friend, that is also distortion at work, where you have interpreted a meaning, which is not the reality. When you lose your keys and look everywhere, and then someone else finds them exactly where you thought they were, but you didn't see them. That's also distortion at work, you believed they were lost.

Filtering through generalisation

This is where we come to our conclusions as we relate and connect new piece of information with something we already know. We associate the new with past experiences. One old poem which so aptly describes how we generalise is *The Blind Men and the Elephant*. Below is the version by John Godfrey Saxe. Each of the blind men imagined and experienced the elephant through the part that they touched and they related it with something that they did know from the past.

> *And so these men of Hindustan*
> *Disputed loud and long,*
> *Each in his own opinion*
> *Exceeding stiff and strong,*
> *Though each was partly in the right*
> *And all were in the wrong.*

The poem begins:
It was six men of Indostan
To learning much inclined,
Who went to see the Elephant (Though all of them were blind),
That each by observation
Might satisfy his mind

They conclude that the elephant is like a wall, snake, spear, tree, fan or rope, depending upon where they touch.

In NLP, to demonstrate how we delete and generalise, we play a game that is similar to any memory game where you have to list 10 items in a particular category. For example, can you rattle off right now 10 different male pop singers? 10 different breakfast options, 10 different luxury car makes, 10 football players, 10 make-up brands? Are you getting it? Did you notice that you can only list a few in the areas that are not of your interest? This is how we read the papers, watch TV and 'listen' to conversations, lectures, how we read books. We only retain the information that gets through our 'Yes/No' filter. The rest is deleted, distorted or generalised.

Dreams

One way of looking at the meaning of your dreams is to see every character as a part of you. Your dreams are not about the people you dream about, but the characteristics and attributes that these people symbolise for you. Leading up to my fortieth birthday, I kept dreaming of male figures and I could not understand it, then I got messages. Everywhere I went I saw the Yin and Yang symbol and the Infinity symbol; both have meanings that point towards the bonding or the co-relation of male and female. I dreamt of drawing this symbol and then I even ended up without any planning at a resort in Bali in May 2011 to celebrate my birthday which had a swimming pool shaped in the infinity shape, with a huge Yin and Yang symbol at the bottom of the pool in the middle.

My friend Simran, a dream interpreter, explained to me how my dreams wanted to remind me to embrace my masculine energy and because I did not see or learn it in my wakeful life, my mind and body had to 'throw bricks at me' so that I would notice in the form of physical signs and dreams. The qualities that I attributed to the men who showed up in these dreams were all the qualities in myself that had been suppressed. I had to learn to harness my assertiveness and my individuality; my personal balance. When you start to notice your dreams and allow them to communicate with you in your waking life, you will notice that everything and everyone in your dream is a representation of you.

Hone your intuition by truly listening and noticing
If you start listening to the sounds around you and truly listen to every conversation you have, aside from making you a better and more compassionate communicator, it will help you absorb a lot more information. Very often when talking to someone, we are either interrupting to speak or we are thinking about what we want to say next; when you truly listen you will get and give so much more to the conversation.

Be aware of your filters and your personal judgements. Being aware as you listen will help you to learn and absorb .

This is the same for what you see. Haven't you noticed when your friend says to you 'Did you see that BMW?' and you didn't? Or times when you say 'Hey, I liked her dress,' and no one else notices it? We habitually only notice, see, hear parts of what is actually present, because of our filters... but we need to practice allowing more to get through. Change your routines and do things you don't normally do, go to new places and see around, even flipping through newspapers and magazines with the intention to find inspiration is a fabulous way to practice it. Instead of looking at your phone when in a car, look outside the window and see, take your environment in, take in nature. Appreciating nature is one of the best ways to experience true gratitude as well.

Think of intuition as tapping on the information that seeped through despite the filters. 'So this is the stuff that I didn't know I knew,' you might say.

Intuition to me is, *knowing on some level.*

I trust that when I am intuitive, it is a cocktail of all the information I have picked up along the way, which has come to me at the right time.

When you are faced with a situation and you are in tune with your intuition, the answer will come to you, from that 'bank'.

You will know when you need to call someone that you care for exactly when they require your love the most. You will know the most appropriate thing to say to someone that you are talking to—even someone you just met. You can start to see the intensity of the intimacy that is achieved in a short period of time. This is called connection sometimes, or rapport.

Trusting your intuition and noticing synchronicity in your life together with your values, your personal declaration and your clearly defined desires will together serve as a navigational compass for you. You will know when to say *No*, where to set boundaries and when to *Go* speeding ahead.

Thinking Pink Synchronicity Exercise
Look at your list of achievements, think of the big epic stories in your life, focus on some of your so-called regrets and list the signs and coincidences that wove them all together. This can be a lot of fun, so take your time with this exercise.

9

Love

Fortune and love favor the brave.
— *Ovid*

If you have skipped to this chapter without reading the earlier ones, I strongly suggest you go back to build your manifesting antenna before reading through this one. Once you have a clear idea of what you want and what you don't, have figured out your personal way to Plug-In, have started practicing watching your thoughts and your language, you have let go of your past, only then can you truly start to manifest anything.

In my years of life coaching, the top three areas that people come to me ready to work on are, often, these very three. So they would want to work on love, their significant relationship if they have one, or on finding someone; they'd want to work on financial goals or turning their passions into businesses; and they would more often than not have a health focus as well, whether it be to lose weight, start meditating, quit smoking or handle pain. In fact I actually believe that our love and money 'valve' are the same, when you open yourself to possibilities, banishing the mentality which says that there isn't enough for all of us, you will open yourself to both.

As Rabii Hillel so aptly said,

If I am not for myself, who will be for me? But if I am only for myself, who am 'I'? And *'If not now, when?*

The word relationship, contextually, usually refers to romantic ones, whereas we must be aware that we are in hundreds of relationships right now. For the sake of clarity in this book, let us refer to one as romantic relationship and the others as all relationships.

Realise that you are in relationships with every member of your family, the company you work in and organisations that you take services from or give services to.

Our soul wants to experience a myriad of emotions and in order to move to a new experience of any intensity or variety, we sometimes have to finish some of the ones we are in presently. We have an underlying desire to manifest a smorgasbord of multiple experiences and that is why we often manifest experiences that we were not expecting.

My most poignant memory of feeling love was when I was a young mother. One afternoon I was sitting on a rocking chair, holding my baby while the Phil Collin's song *'Groovy kind of love'* was playing. I was feeding her and I remember the tears and boundless love I felt cradling my precious, soft, clad-in-white little angel in my arms. The lyrics 'when I'm in your arms, nothing seems to matter, my whole world can shatter, I don't care, wouldn't you agree, baby you and me, gotta groovy kind of love' mesmerised me to no known extent. I can still remember the smell of her baby skin.

Love is everywhere and there are so many ranges of love. I manifest love all day and every day. *I love*. Waiting for that one person or that eternal love in order to feel complete is adopting a lack mentality around love and it will close you off to gratitude of the love you do have, making it impossible to attract more love.

The only way to find the right relationship is to first be happy being single. It's about emotional independence and being happy and grateful for the love you already have around you. Like with everything else, be grateful for all the love that surrounds you. Don't be afraid to call it love. The more you love, the more loving you are, the more love you will manifest in your life. No one goes around saying 'Love me', we say 'I Love You', to be loved, to *find* love, be loving.

When you can find your own axis, you can revolve around it, for when you revolve your life on someone outside of you, you lose your own alignment. Just as the earth revolves around its own axis daily and through this eternal gentle revolving it also revolves around the sun, if you don't find your own axis and you don't gently revolve, you cannot be for anyone.

Then, once you have centred on your axis and someone else who has also centred on theirs is brought into your world, the two of you can come together and there is a collision of axes and you shift from your centre. This is the sensation of 'falling in love'.

If, after the initial combustion, you can realign so that you can revolve on your own axis and simultaneously rotate with the other body, then you may have found a true and balanced way of relating; thus, a healthy relationship. You maintain and grow your individuality as you serve the world as well and live your own purpose whilst simultaneously relating lovingly with another.

Yes, many of you reading this chapter want it to be about manifesting that one romantic love you desire and I will share many ways you can do just that. However, I have to stress that life is not about achieving this one eternal love, but to be gracious about all the people who love you now. Be present to what you have. If you have parents, remember how much they love you. If you are still harbouring any pain around them, forgive them and ask them for their forgiveness. If there is someone who cooks for you, realise that this is love too; if you are lucky enough to come home to a dog wagging its tail on your arrival, you have the purest form of love there is. Totally unconditional and free of ego, kick it him away and it will still come back for more of your 'loving'.

You may love many, many people in your lifetime and many people will love you back, too. Think of all the people you care about and the ones who care about you, at home, at work, in your neighbourhood. Learn to extract all the positive experiences and gifts that you got from all these relationships, even the romantic ones that didn't end up lasting your lifetime.

Love is empathy and compassion

A praise of compassion by Lama Zopa Rinpoche:

Live with compassion.
Work with compassion.
Die with compassion.
Meditate with compassion.
Enjoy with compassion.
When problems come,
Experience them with compassion.

The definition of compassion is: wanting others to be free from suffering.

If you have been lucky enough to be around children, wide-eyed, curious and so trusting, then you have experienced love. I used to teach English as a second language when I lived in Indonesia and although at that time I had already had my daughter, I remember the gratitude and astounding love I felt every day from these kids. At the time, I did not call it gratitude, I just felt it. Love abounds around us all, if we are only vulnerable enough to let it. Vulnerability is the willingness to let it in and to feel.

I used to enjoy watching 'Vampire Diaries', a TV show where the breathtakingly-debonair vampire Damon explained how they had to 'switch off' feeling so that they could kill for blood, but when they did that they switched off, allowing love in as well. Many of us have switched off, even some of us in relationships and marriages, we become desensitised because we don't want to be disappointed or hurt by our partners. Living in India, people switch off from the poverty around so as not to feel sad, because we think we can't do anything. But there were people like Mother Theresa who kept saying, 'every drop helps'. The invitation is to open your heart, open the floodgates and let it all in. *The joy, gratitude and love that will flow in will surpass any fear or sadness that you wanted to keep out.*

To open yourself to receiving, you have to give and in order to give you have to care. What do you care about and who do you care about? The first list that you may come up with is your family, partner, your children, parents and siblings, and then your friends and the people you work with. Who else do you care about?

What if you believed that you have been strategically placed by the Universe to care about all the people you have already come in contact with and that you are an instrument not only of your wealth, but your knowledge, time and your love?

Who can you be compassionate to, today?

The good thing about sadness is that it allows for empathy. When something can move you, you know that you care. When you have been unconscious or oblivious to lack or suffering around you, it is not because you don't care, but rather because you have had filters in place to protect you from the sadness that it invokes. First up, being empathetic does not mean that you have to solve the problems of the world, it starts with just trying to understand them.

All the peace and happiness of the whole globe, the peace and happiness of societies, the peace and happiness of family, the peace and happiness in the individual persons' life, and the peace and happiness of even the animals and so forth, all depends on having loving kindness toward each other.

—Lama Zopa Rinpoche

Listen and give your full attention. If you have found the time to talk to someone, then you have to have the time and energy to listen to them attentively. Notice your judgments and filters and how you may be comparing your own problems and heartaches to theirs. Try not to relate your own situations with theirs to discount their plight. This is an understandably common reaction when you are talking to someone who you feel is so much more blessed and fortunate than you, in that they have more resources or they seem to be living some of the desires that you are still manifesting.

If you are struggling financially and one of your wealthy friends is upset about the way their parents are talking to them or how their friends take advantage of them, don't get angry and blame the person for their own problems. This is the opposite of empathy. Yes, their set of cards are different from yours, but they need empathy, too.

There's no pain big or small, pain is equal and to be truly empathetic, you have to be able to feel it from their point of view, understanding where they are coming from.

Have you spoken to children and heard them complaining about their exams and being tired from their school, sports and social schedules and their friends having issues with them? Have you ever listened in on the conversation teen-aged girls have about boys, that of jealousy and their self image? Often we trivialise their plight, thinking we have bigger problems and real responsibilities. And we scoff at these kids for being stressed over such nonsense. Empathy is putting that judgment aside and truly listening to these kids, knowing how significant, big and real these issues are to them and making an effort to understand.

Have you flicked through the newspapers and seen so much news of death, poverty, war, mishaps and then instead of reading through it, you skim it and look for happier images and news, or news that is relevant to you? This is your natural self-preservation again, protecting you from feeling bad or sad.

As much as it is crucial that you do focus on the images and things and thoughts you want to manifest in your life, equally important is to care and feel some empathy for people who have so much less than you do. Don't even go so far as the local or international news; open yourself up to all the people you meet daily and start caring. Put yourself in their shoes and truly imagine what their lives, their homes, their problems and their desires could be—that is empathy, which can be expressed with compassion.

As His Holiness The Dalai Lama (XIV) said in *The Compassionate Life*:

Compassion without attachment is possible. Therefore, we need to clarify the distinctions between compassion and attachment. True compassion is not just an emotional response but a firm commitment founded on reason. Because of this firm foundation, a truly compassionate attitude toward others does not change even if they behave negatively. Genuine compassion is based not on our own projections and expectations, but rather on the needs of the other: irrespective of whether another person is a close friend or an enemy, as long as that person wishes for peace and happiness and wishes to overcome suffering, then on that basis we develop genuine concern for their problem. This is genuine compassion.

'(For a Buddhist practitioner) The goal is to develop this genuine compassion, this genuine wish for the well-being of another, in fact for every living being throughout the universe.'

Start practicing empathy and compassion immediately. The first step is to listen with love. Compassion for others can only attract more love into your life. Open your heart to give and to receive.

Romantic love
Being deeply loved by someone gives you strength, while loving someone deeply gives you courage.

— *Lau Tzu*

Being grateful and truly relishing all the love you already have in your life is not contradictory to still wanting to manifest romantic love. Your soul wants to experience romantic love as well.

Before you can manifest, you have to decide which side of the fence you want to be on, at least for now. As an old

Jewish saying goes, 'You can't dance in two weddings at the same time.' So if it is a long-term commitment you are seeking, wait for it and play the rules; but if it is casual dating you want for now, then set a time-frame and stick by it.

Of the 6 basic human needs, derived from Maslow's hierarchy of needs, two of them are Certainty and Uncertainty. Human beings need both. We need certainty, so we can trust and depend on certain structures, beliefs and people. And we need uncertainty, so we can experience adventure and not feel bored. So in this conversation it is normal to want a casual date for a while and then suddenly reassess and desire something more substantial.

When you have decided that it is a long-term committed relationship you want to manifest, then the first thing to do is understand that the Universe is huge and that there are plenty of wonderful men and women out there who you could have a wonderful life with. Men and women complain about the same things, with their negative beliefs in mind, that there are no women in this town, all the single guys are taken, I am too old to find someone now. Quit that and look around you and see the sea of single people who are looking for the same thing out there. Men and women behave the way we expect them to or the way we accept them behaving. The same person who could have been a jerk to you could make someone else a loving, caring, respectful and honest spouse. So before you go on your self-sabotaging mission about being right rather than being happy, before you go out there affirming that all men are lying b******** and all women are manipulative b******, realise that they are only being who you expect them to be and they will continue to behave the way you accept them behaving.

The Universe wants you to have what you desire. So be patient and detach yourself from the outcome of these relationships; the same goes with money.

Being needy, pushy and trying to force a relationship does not work and it is horribly unattractive. Stop looking at every man or woman you meet as a possible partner. This will limit your manifesting abilities. Allow yourself to be guided.

If things do not work out the way you wanted or hoped, it is fine. Move on, being grateful for the lessons and the experience, which would have altered you a little at least and, perhaps, groomed you for the next opportunity. I have had my share of heartaches and disappointments in this area and I keep at it, manifesting love all the time, as should you.

Manifesting Romantic Love Steps

\# **Visualise**—Use the Jigsaw Puzzle Visualisation Exercise and imagine yourself in a loving embrace with someone. Remember not to have a specific face or identity. You cannot limit the Universe.

\# **Say Affirmations** and positive statements, as if you already have it. Example of some affirmations for love:

I am grateful to have this wonderful relationship based on love and respect with my loving, confident, spiritual man/ woman; where we just love to be together because there is a lot of expansion, fun and amazing sex.

\# **Write out the qualities** you want your man or woman to have, using the Partner Shopping List exercise at the end of this chapter, keeping in mind on a subconscious level that the one you want may not be exactly the one you have in mind. Your higher self knows what it wants, though your conscious self may be obsessed or fixated on something else which is in your visibility range. This is just your impatience of wanting to settle for less, because you are afraid of the unknown. Make sure you use the technique in chapter 1 and only state these attributes in positive language.

The Universe manifests but we should not stop its action by requesting for a particular person, rather focus on the qualities we want this person to have and how we want to feel when we are with them.

Feel—How you think you will feel when you are with this person. Imagine the conversations, embrace and the pure joy that you will experience when with this person. By feeling it in the now, the man or woman manifests exactly as we want them to be.

Give Up Control—Allow: If you have a mental visual or even a physical vision board, in which you have imagined the face or reference of a specific person you want to 'make-yours', you need to remove it and replace it with a faceless and nameless person. Don't try to control anything that you desire, instead give up all the control, manifest gracefully and give space to the Universe to allow.

A client of mine who was quite visual and used to diligently update her vision board since the desires she had put up images for had started to manifest in her life, told me how she had stuck images of the man she wanted to 'make-hers' and she was fixated on the relationship going the way she wanted it to. The man was just not right for her and she didn't see that. Finally, she trusted me and she replaced all his pictures with the image of a male figure that was indistinct. She gave up her need to control and limit the Universe from sending into her life people that would far better match her desires, who would allow her to meet her own full potential. She said to me, 'When I removed his photo from my board, the right man appeared.'

\# **Trust the Universe implicitly**—Know in the deepest part of your body and mind that love is making its way to you and will only come when you are both ready. Imagine that all the other encounters you have are preparing you with the lessons you need to learn, so that you will be attractive to this person you want to attract. And you will already have grown and evolved enough to be with this person.

Trust that just as you have made a list and have a vision of this wonderful relationship, so do other people, even if they do not believe or practice this on a conscious level. Practicing on a conscious level would take you to a higher pedestal.

\# **Watch your visualisation** often and imagine the image of you and your partner floating up like a balloon into the sky. Imagine that the Universe is your personal match-making site and it is waiting for all the possible matches to become apparent or to be ready. And then, once the matches are made, these people will magically appear into your world.

\# Speak to five people you know who found love recently and acknowledge the serendipitous circumstances that brought them together.

Be discerning

Once you start manifesting, you will have to practice being discerning. The Universe will send many contenders and one or more than one could be likely candidates. Unfortunately, the only way to find out is to allow yourself to get to know them. Some qualities that you desire may be present but not evident immediately, so you need to trust that you need to meet these people safely, to get to know them more closely. When it feels right in your gut, embrace it fully.

When your contenders show up, know what you want and then check the person against your wish-list. If there is a match and if, instinctively, you think you want to explore the possibility of a relationship, communicate it and be clear, since when two people who want different things meet, often there can be pain and disappointment. This is why it is important for both men and women to give out clear signals and communicate honestly.

In my years as a life coach many women, even when they say they are happy being casual, are actually just bartering sex for love; they are hoping that the casual physical relationship will grow into mutual love, but it does not. More often than not the men that they indulge with are also looking for a long-term relationship but till they find that girl, they want to have sex as much as they can with as many women as they can. So if it does feel like you are banging your head against the wall trying too hard to make something happen, it would be wise to stop and step back.

Men also have various reasons that come in the way of committing. Some have been hurt deeply by past relationships and find it hard to trust again, so they 'take what they can get' in the meantime. Whether you are a man or a woman, knowing what you want and sending out clear signals will attract it back to you. When you are not sure about what you want, you may attract all sorts of attention. And when you become clear about what you don't want, the unwanted attention will stop. Then, when you stop accepting what you don't want and you are not willing to settle for less, you will start to attract only exactly what you want.

You can't lie to the Universe; it will give you what you want, so be sure that every part of you is aligned and you are sending out the same order. Behaving in ways that are not aligned with what you desire will have its consequences and only delay your truest desires from having the space to manifest. It is like nodding your head but saying 'no'. Your 'order' and your actions have to be aligned. Remembering to Plug In often will support you in being able to send clear signals.

Love the one you are with

If you are already with the person you love or you have found her/him recently, then keeping the love is what you want to manifest. A relationship should be looked at as a verb, not a noun, how you choose to relate every single moment with a significant other person. It is a verb—continuous—you are in a relationship for as long as you are relating with this person. And if you are doing it lovingly then you are in a good relationship.

Whose responsibility is a relationship? 50-50? 80-20?

Each partner has to give 100% in order for a relationship to work. The first thing to let go of is the need for another person in our lives to make us happy. Remember the axis?

A real, loving relationship is a partnership of mutual support, mutual pleasure and mutual respect. Relationships are 'created' and don't exist until two people unite in a common purpose. You make a choice to continue to relate with another person in a loving and conducive way so that each of you can meet your life goals and attain personal growth.

Remember why you are in the relationship in the first place. To me, the only reason to be in one is because you undeniably want to be in it; being there gives you joy. We have a choice every single moment to decide and choose what we want. There are no 'have-tos'. The minute you feel you have to be where you are, you are imposing compulsions on yourself and taking away all the joy. Why be in a committed relationship? Or why get married? When you are clear about our own personal reasons, then you have chosen it out of a 'want' and not a 'have-to'.

You will not have anything to complain about. You won't be complaining about your situation or your partner. Learning to respond with your 'reason for choosing to be together' in mind, rather than reacting angrily or defensively to each other, is essential. You want 'to relate with this person lovingly everyday'. So the next time your partner pushes your buttons or says something that almost invokes an impulsive reaction (which you know is going to cause a war), wait and think about why you are in this relationship again. Some may say, 'We're stuck together because of children, culture, family, society or security'. Well, you are not stuck, you are still making a choice to stay in it because the consequences may be too high to pay. If you are choosing to be together, for whatever reason, remember it is still your choice and you might as well make it a loving co-existence than resist it every minute of the day. Remember the 3 manholes?

Developing the habit of carefully choosing our responses, instead of impulsively reacting to each other, is different from letting your partner walk all over you. No one wants to be a doormat, or be involved in a relationship with a pushover. Learning to love, and cultivating good relationship skills, means understanding your own place in your life. Choosing a response that is sensitive to the feelings of your partner is a priceless habit to form in order to have a happy and loving relationship. There is a delicate balance between giving freely and thinking of our own needs. This is the trickiest relationship skill to master, but perhaps the most rewarding.

As Viktor Frankl said:

Between stimulus and response there is a space. In that space is our power to choose our response. In our response lies our growth and our freedom.

Thinking Pink Partner Shopping List Exercise
Similar to the exercise we did in Chapter 1, this one is specific to attracting the partner you desire into your life.

Make your list of what you don't want in a partner, then cross out the don't wants and replace them with its polar opposite to discover what you do want. Be careful not to get into details of how and where, focus on the end quality. Look back at your list of values and list the values you are looking for in your partner, they may not be identical to yours, but there may be some that are truly important to you. Think about the feeling you want, not just the aesthetics; most of the happiest and most intimate couples I have met are not married to the physical equivalent of Brad Pitt or Angelina Jolie.

Use thoughts of past relationships or relationships of the people you have seen in your circle, including your parents' marriage, to identify the things you want and do not want. For example, if you added to your 'don't want list' someone who is 'controlling' and 'loud', you will strike through 'controlling' and 'loud', then write 'easy-going' and 'soft spoken' on the right side of the table.

WORKABLES

Make a list of issues you know you can compromise on. These are things that may irritate you but you know you can live with. It all comes with relating to another person and sharing your space with her/him. For example: 'She's messy, but I can live with that', We can hire a cleaner.

PERSONAL ADJUSTMENTS

The second step is to make a list of issues you would compromise on within yourself for another person.

DON'T WANTS	WANTS
~~Controlling~~	Easy Going
~~Loud~~	Soft Spoken

'I know I'm messy, so I'd either get an organiser to help me with this or be willing to hire a housekeeper.'

ABSOLUTE NON-NEGOTIABLES

Make a list of issues you could not and would not compromise on. The list should focus on daily issues.

If you're not sure how to identify the non-negotiable, ask yourself this question:

If this behaviour never changed, could I live with it?

You have to assume it may never change and that alone should help you determine if it's a negotiable or non-negotiable.

Emotional intimacy

Anytime we care deeply about or fall in love with somebody or something, we give away some power over our feelings. It is impossible to love without giving away some power. We are vulnerable, which is not a bad thing, though make sure that you are not giving up who you are.

A common thing that happens in the early stages of young relationships is that the two of you start to emulate each other and want to please each other. You suddenly start to change some of your own likes and dislikes to match the other person's. Favourite songs and food are sometimes forgotten and replaced. There is a fine line between being accommodating and caring versus giving up your sense of self. If your partner inspires you to change some of your habits which were disempowering and unhealthy then that's great; if you learn to do some things differently so as to have a more peaceful relationship, that is also great. There is a difference between giving up who you are just to be with this person and making some changes out of love.

As a verb 'intimate' means 'to state or make known'. 'Into-me-you-see.'

Intimacy is to be able to be our true and authentic self when we are in a relationship and allow the other person to do the same.

'Being ourselves' requires that we can talk openly about things that are important to us, emotionally and sexually and that we are comfortable to stand up for our personal preferences, our values and set our boundaries.

'Allowing the other person to do the same' is the willingness to remain emotionally tied to someone who has different thoughts, values, preferences and boundaries. Wanting to change the other person is not intimacy.

If you use the analogy of 'dancing', when you start to change your steps and your moves and your partner picks up your nuances and starts to dance with you, that is making responsible and lasting changes that enhance your capacity for genuine closeness over the long haul. It is not about changing the other person, which is not possible; it is, though, about changing yourself. What you are willing to accept in the other person and how autonomous you are willing to be in the relationship.

Often, we fear being independent at the risk of losing the other. We have to have faith that the relationship is serving them as much as it is serving us. The fear of losing the partner is often mutual. And when there is love, our need for each other is usually mutual. So, have faith in the love.

Don't keep secrets; in a relationship where trust is the main glue, make sure there are never areas that you cannot talk about. This is the quickest way to kill intimacy. This is different from telling your partner every single detail about your past or your past relationships. If you have forgiven yourself and accepted all of your past then they are resolved and do not need to come into this relationship. Infidelity, however, is a killer of any real and trusting relationship and it is not even just about the sexual indiscretion, it is about all the lies and betrayal that is needed to carry it on.

Love strategies

I am going to share with you a magical NLP secret. Something you wish you knew long ago. It is so simple and many of you guys out there would be wishing you had this sort of 'cheat sheet' on all the girls you ever went out with.

So here it is:

Think of a time you felt truly and completely like you were being loved.

Was it something you heard, saw or felt?

A couple, John and Jane, went in to see a hypnotist for some marriage counseling. They were feeling like they had lost the magic in their relationship and they were a couple that were once 'madly in love' with each other. So, the hypnotist asked John first to think of a time when he felt like he was truly and completely being loved.

'Think of a time, perhaps in your childhood.'

Was it something you heard being said to you? A touch? A gesture?'

John answered that he felt loved when

1. He heard the words, 'I love you, John' He loved hearing his own name being uttered out loud.

2. He also felt loved when he was cooked for, when he knew that the woman he adored cared enough to go to the shops, buy ingredients, chop, marinate and spend time and effort in the kitchen for the sheer pleasure of satisfying his palate.

3. When someone ran their hands through his scalp, his hair, almost scratching with nails, through the top of his head, the neck, the sides of his head, he felt cared for, nurtured, loved...adored.

Jane was asked the same question and she said that she felt truly loved when

1. She heard the words 'you are so beautiful, Jane' whispered in her ear. Her name being said to her made her feel loved.

2. When she was given thoughtful gifts, flowers or chocolate, basically when someone spent their precious time and money on her. She wanted to know that they were willing to give up something precious to make her feel good.

3. When she was held firmly around her waist and kissed on her neck. Especially from behind her. Her waist was a pressure point that made her feel sexy, feminine, beautiful and desirable. She felt like she could lose herself in wild abandon and relish in the sensations of pleasure and hedonistic satisfaction when held that way.

When either of them felt, saw or heard these things, they were like 'buttons' being pushed which made them feel loved. When they first met, as most new lovers, both were randomly doing everything for the other as you do in the early stages of a relationship.

So, by default, they happened to press the right buttons as well, unknowingly, of course, like a child pressing all the floors in the elevator and hitting the right floor in the process.

So, by 'mistake' John was holding Jane's waist from behind her and facing her, he was holding her hips, too, and her shoulders, too, but he got the waist sometimes, just like even a broken clock gets the time right twice a day!

Jane, too, was hitting the spots when she ran her fingers through John's scalp and his back and arms as well, she too got it right a few times.

The thing, though, is that after a relationship gets over the honeymoon stage, we humans tend to become comfortable and then we relax and revert to either not pressing buttons, or maybe pressing our own 'buttons' on our partners.

So what was happening in John and Jane's case is that, of late, John was saying, 'I love you' to Jane and he even cooked for them some nights. And Jane would hold John around the waist and buy him stuff. Both of them were 'missing the spot.'

Think about having an itch on your back and having your hands tied up holding a heavy box in front of you, and you ask your partner to scratch it for you and they just can't seem to scratch the itch, missing it by centimetres all the time. This can be so frustrating.

They had both reverted to their own 'love strategies' and unfortunately this left the other feeling totally unfulfilled, lonely and unloved. If you knew how easy and almost effortless it would be to make the person you love feel good, wouldn't you just do it? Especially when you were aware of the good feelings it would invoke in the other and therefore infuse back to you?

It sounds so easy and almost mechanical, but it is so effective and not doing it can be so detrimental to the relationship. I have had people ask me why their partners don't instinctively know what to do to give them joy and that it takes the romance away if you have to tell them, but I think that if you are going to wait around for someone to come along that is 'special' because he or she happens to be familiar with the particular brand of love strategy you desire, you may miss out on the one that is right for you, when all you need to do is communicate.

Tip for the women:

This was shared with me by one of my coaches, treat your man as if he were a tree. You and your children, sit under the tree in its shade. Nurture the tree, and it will grow, give the tree space to spread its branches and ground its roots and it will bear sweet, luscious fruit and a thick and protective shade. The fruits will fall for our children and us and we get to bask in the love and security of the shade.

Tip for the men:

My doctor back in Sydney, Isaac, once held out a bunch of pens and pencils to me and asked me to take one out to give to him. I did and then he handed me the whole bunch telling me that in his years of experience with women and couples, he knew without a doubt that, if a man gave a woman a single gesture of love, she would reciprocate by giving him her all, she will shower you with love and affection like you never knew she was capable of.

Trust your partner

Simply put, intimacy, love and trust go together. In order to be intimate (physically, emotionally or spiritually), we have to let our guard down and be vulnerable. This requires a sense of emotional safety on both sides and a belief that our partner will not betray or intentionally hurt us.

If you doubt your partner, it will come through in anything you say. You will be insinuating doubt and suspicion, which will make the other feel un-trusted. The easiest way to sabotage your relationship or marriage is to simply not trust your partner.

By trust I am referring to all levels of trust not, just fidelity.

Trusting your partner with money and decisions. Trusting your spouse to look after your kids competently. Trusting that they care about you enough to respect your wishes and not abuse you in any way.

How to build trust in your relationship?

Learn to communicate effectively
In a disagreement, many people spend their time thinking about what they are going to say, rather than listening closely to understand the perspective of their partner. Or, they get caught up in the intense emotions of the moment, which usually disables their ability to hear what the other is saying.

When emotions are flaring, we also tune out, thinking the other is being irrational and that anything that is being said will be retracted later. There could be some truth in this, so listen, but be sure not to take anything said in the heat of the moment to heart and never use it to throw back at your partner.

Give each other time and space and the freedom to deal with the matter in their own way.

So guys, the next time your girlfriend/wife goes running to her mother or friends to talk about you, just know that it is the equivalent of you going into your study to play with your Wii or Nintendo for a few hours.

Ask for what you want clearly and allow each other to say 'no' without guilt

Don't expect your partner to read your mind; if you want them to do something, ask them specifically for what you want. Remember that you are two people brought up in different homes and with different habits and values and to assume that the other should KNOW how and what you want is ridiculous. Never assume that anything is common-knowledge.

When you are uncomfortable or simply do not want to do something, be lovingly firm and say 'no'. Allow your partner to say 'no' without repercussions, too. Even if you are disappointed, accept that you are better off being slightly disappointed than having the person you love lie or pretend to you. A distorted internal link most of us have is to connect the 'No' to a request to meaning a 'No' to yourself. We take the rejection personally, which is misplaced.

Be your word – keep your promises

Mean what you say and say what you mean. Remember that communication is made up of only 5 per cent of the words we utter, the rest of it is: our tone, body language and facial expressions. Even if your partner may not be able to articulate it, they will know when you are not being congruent.

When you say you are going to be home at a certain time, mean it. When you both always do as you say you will do, trust grows. It is the little things that add up. Set reminders in your phone, get your secretary or kid to remind you to, but always do as you say you are going to do. If you agreed to buy milk on the way home, or pick up his dry-cleaning, do so. Take away the need to be reminded or nagged. Can you see how powerful this can be, for a partner to KNOW that something is going to be done just because their partner SAID so?

If you can build this through repeated small actions, then when big re-assurances or promises are uttered, both partners will have faith that it will come to pass.

Have faith that your partner wants the relationship to work as much as you do and that they are as strong as you are. 'But, I don't want to hurt him/her.' That is an assumption that they are not as strong!

Your partner has the internal strength to be in a relationship of mutual respect and equality. If you don't trust her/his intelligence and strength, s/he will pick up on it and often take on that role so as to avoid confrontation. When we give our partner the truth and we respect that they can handle it, we are empowering him/her.

Thinking Pink Listing the Endearing Qualities Exercise

This is the same as the Antagonist exercise at the end of chapter 5.

Think of your existing partner, or any person you are in any kind of relationship with, that you feel is causing you discomfort, irritability or resentment and start listing *only* their endearing qualities.

Love Tips

Waiting for that eternal love in order to feel complete is adopting a lack mentality around love and will close you off to gratitude of the love you do have.

- # Practice empathy and compassion daily.
- # Visualise.
- # Say Affirmations.
- # Feel.
- # Trust the Universe Implicitly.

Surrender and renounce the attachment to your desire and truly be grateful and nurture all your other loving relationships. And as you read in the previous chapter, love abounds us and feeling lonely or unloved just because you have not found the one companion to share your entire tomorrows with is rejecting the love that is already around you.

10

Wealth and Health

The first wealth is health.
— Ralph Waldo Emerson

What is wealth to you?

There is no fixed definition of wealth. Everyone has their own perception of it.

Some say wealth is being happy, it means having friends and loved ones who truly care about you and you about them. Being able to afford the time to get to do the things you truly want to do is to be wealthy.

We are the most fortunate species as we are the only ones who can experience so many facets of emotion, pleasures, joy and love. When we desire and manifest abundance, we become more equipped to support others.

For those of us who are blessed enough to be able to afford to even buy books and the education we received to be able to read, it is our duty and responsibility to help the less fortunate. No matter how wealthy or how poor you believe yourself to be, there is an amount of money or resources that you could easily give which, in parting with it, would not make much of a difference to your lifestyle, but would mean food, shelter, healthcare or education to so many. Care.

Many of us have desensitised ourselves to the suffering around us. Just thinking about it makes many of us uncomfortable and helpless and because of the perceived helplessness, we block out the entire thought. Many of us feel that because we can't change the world, what's the point of thinking about of it. We imagine that any help we feel we can offer would be like a drop in the ocean and therefore futile, but every little morsel does make a difference.

Before you read on, think about just one person you think you can help and one charitable organisation that you can support. The sharing of wealth, coming from being compassionate and generous, is the spiritual side of manifesting wealth.

Contentment is natural wealth, luxury is artificial poverty.
— *Socrates*

Money is energy. It does not come to you to stay, it comes through you to flow to other people and in the process it enriches your life in the ways you want.

In order to manifest wealth you have to find something you love passionately. I say 'passionately' but this is the kind of love that other people can view as 'obsessively'. When you start loving something so much and give it your all, the money energy will just flow in.

In the Bhagwad Gita, Chapter 2, it is said

Be focused on action and not on the fruits of action. Do not become confused in attachment to the fruit of your actions and do not become confused in the desire for inaction (2.47).

When I was going through my journey of trying to keep afloat, I was lucky enough to meet Diana Cooper, who is a spiritual teacher in Pune, India. She shared her personal mantra with mantra with me; 'I am, I know I am, the use of God's limitless opulence and supply.'

If 'God' does not sit well with you yet, then replace God with 'The Universe'.

This mantra changed my life and I hope it does the same for you.

Every time we receive cash or cheques or any kind of abundance, say it and feel it, feel the money energy flowing through you and know that you are just the instrument and that the money has come to you to flow through you to someone else and, in the process, leave with you some of the Opulence of the Universe, which is a limitless flow.

Money passes through us to move elsewhere. Don't be fixated on how or where the money will come to you, but rather on what you are doing each day and, even while you sleep, what you want to create in your experience and it will come to you.

Being open to the 'wherefroms' and the 'hows', gives the Universe the freedom to send it to you to flow through you to wherever else the energy needs to flow to. Focus on the experience and the way you want to feel, not on the monetary number and then do all you can to give to the Universe.

Vision board and flow list

Think of all the reasons you want money. All the things you don't want and all the things you want that you feel money will give to you. As usual, re-word all your 'don't wants' into wants just like we did in Chapter 1 and 9.

If you don't want to be in debt, don't want to drive your old car, don't want to always have to look at the price when ordering food, don't want to travel economy, don't want to feel scared about your future, don't want to be billed heavily by surprise, don't want to always be scraping to pay rent, rewrite all these with what you want. As you do this, notice how much of it you already have, how much more you have than most of the world. Feel the gratitude as you create your vision and feel it every time you look at it.

Think of all the material things you want. Don't be shy, let it flow, go through the newspapers every morning and the glossy fashion, travel and business magazines and tear out the words or images of the luxuries you want to experience. You can also do this digitally, if you prefer, by creating a word document and pasting all the images of the situations and things you desire. Remember that I said 'experience' and not own.

If you want to always live in an opulent space, you can easily have it. It may not be your own, but the Universe could give you ample opportunities to enjoy it. Look at this picture often and add or change the words and images when you think of new experiences you desire. Include images that symbolise the people you want to help and what you will be giving them; so, for example, if you want to contribute to the education of children, find an image that depicts that to you. If it is housing or medical supplies that you want to give, then find images that would symbolise that. If you already have a charity or a family that you contribute to, then add the image or words that will mirror that.

This reminds me of a time, a few years ago, when I had just started writing this book and I honestly wanted to experience opulent and luxurious living at a higher-than-5-star hotel level and at that point I had never ever travelled business class. I also wanted to always go up on a Hot Air Balloon.

It was really interesting how quickly all these desires became real for me and in the most unexpected ways 'through' the least expected people. I was flying from Mumbai to Dubai and as I reached the check-in counter, the Cathay Pacific flight attendant simply asked me, 'Ms Bhojwani, would you mind if we upgraded you to Business Class?' Would I mind? Apart from the champagne, the best thing about the experience for me was the polite service and being addressed all night as Ms Bhojwani. I simply loved it and nowadays, in my personal visualisation, I add that into the soundtrack.

Recently I was in Singapore and was booked to come back to Mumbai on economy and I had one of the Business Class baggage tags lying with me. Spoilt from the previous experiences, I willed it to happen again, so I slept with the tag on my nightstand on top of my TAG Journal and the next day, my uncle Sajan, who wanted me to carry some heavy packages back to Mumbai for him, asked me if I would, and I said that being on Economy, I would be happy to but didn't have the baggage allowance, so he picked up the phone in front of me and because we shared the same last name, he easily got me upgraded and this time it was on Singapore Airlines, so I got to experience more champagne and more of the 'Ms Bhojwani' service.

I was invited to present at an International Coach Federation (ICF) Conference in Bangalore on 'The Law Of Attraction' and I booked myself into the decent but very average hotel that the conference was being held at. However a close friend's family, who was also inspired by the work I did, insisted on extending hospitality to me and said that they would have invited me to stay at their home, but because they were renovating, there was no space. So, they put me up at The

Leela, which was one of the most opulent experiences I have ever had. When I dreamt of luxury, I had always seen visuals of rose petals floating on water and the entire hotel lobby and driveway had large pots with fresh rose petals in them.

At that stage I had already started practicing expressing my gratitude, so all this went into my journal in detail and the gratitude of opulence and abundance only brings in more and more. A huge blockage of manifesting wealth is ingratitude and dissatisfaction. Let's say you need $5000 for something and you are practicing the manifestation techniques, you are open to receiving and you are seeing and feeling that you have that experience you want, and then you find 10c on the floor and someone deposits $20 in your bank account and then a friend asks you to hold on to $200 for them and another friend invites you to dinner. But instead of being grateful for all this abundance flowing into your life, you remain annoyed and dissatisfied that you have not seen your $5000. You are then repeating a mantra in your head subconsciously that this is not enough, I will never get enough, when is it going to come right? What do you think this line of ingratitude and mantras are going to attract into your experience? Yes, more that is not enough. Even beggars on the street understand this principle; when they beg from car to car and receive mere coins, they don't fling the coins back at you, they bless you and they move on to the next car.

Even charities or causes trying to raise half a million dollars will not express ingratitude to the donor who offers them a few hundred dollars. It all adds up, it is about the energy and vibrations you exude, filled with deep and authentic gratitude. The only way to conquer the ingratitude is to have utter faith that more will come.

The daily practice of gratitude is one of the conduits by which your wealth will come to you.
  — Wallace Wattles (1860-1911), The Science Of Getting Rich

After my *Gratitude Journal* was published, someone wrote in asking me: was it wrong, selfish or manipulative to only write in gratitude because you believed that it would then bring you more? My answer to that was, you cannot fake gratitude, so even if you are practicing it because of your own self-satisfying reasons, you are practicing it and you will grow to become more and more grateful as you manifest more and more abundance in your life.

Another killer of the abundance flow is envy and jealousy. Notice anything you feel or say to yourself when you see others who have what you want and desire. If you find yourself habitually going into a negative conversation with yourself when you see someone driving a car you like, wearing a new piece of jewellery or sharing with the world the amazing holidays they went on, stop there and immediately change the talk to that of appreciation. Appreciate, admire and desire what they have and be happy that they already have it; all this should do is reinforce to you that your manifestations can and will work as well.

Think and then feel the feelings you will have when you have all your financial dreams come true. Connect to the feeling and try not to attach to the details or the way you will experience these feelings and, I promise you, you will manifest the situations to help you feel the exact way you want to.

Next, make a list of what you want to do with all the financial abundance you desire, you need to create and carve out the flow-out channel and it has to lead to enhancing the lives of other people. Like I said in Chapter 1, this does not have to be an altruistic list, just trust that just by having the experience and abundance you desire, millions of people will also benefit and have what they desire. Remember to add to this list the charity organisation and names of people you want to help financially. If you can't think of one, then enrol a group of your friends and contacts and agree to form a cause and contribute an amount every month. If you put your heart and desires collectively to this, this could grow and be of benefit to hundreds, maybe thousands, of people.

Educate yourself on wealth and finances and increase your vocabulary to what it would be like when you have manifested these desires. A simple way to do this is to imagine you have won a lottery and list how you would 'spend' your winnings. Realise, too, that the Universe is opulent and abundant; It may have so much more in store for you than you can even fathom or imagine; so, always leave some ambiguity in your list.

Money is not evil

What if you truly believed, instead, that 'Money flows to me naturally by my service to others'?

We can't make money; unless we had a mint or we worked at the Bureau of Engraving and Printing, we have to earn our money. To earn means to give value in return for energy. Any service or product that you provide in exchange for money is earning. To take this a step further, if it weren't for you earning money, how would the world go around?

I attended a big Indian wedding in a resort island recently and I overheard people saying the typical 'What a criminal waste of money' looking at the flowers, the food, décor and fashion display. However, my thought was, WOW, look at the abundance and gifts that this wedding has provided the local community of this island with! The florists earned money, the restaurants and caterers earned money, the bellhops earned their tips, the designers and tailors earned and all this creates more money, 'abundance'. Are you with me so far? The wealthy family's luxurious wedding, at an island resort that was not normally familiar to seeing such display of wealth or such a high demand of service, 'boosted the economy' of this island. The hairdressers, who had little shops that serviced five to eight women a day, were commissioned to coiffeur the tresses of over two hundred women every day for over three days. All the locals earned much more than they did annually in these three days and in turn also spent on the services that they required, paying for their food and their kid's education and their livelihoods, so fulfilling their passions and needs. Never feel guilty for your spending; if you are among the lucky who have more money energy flowing through your life, then allow it to flow out generously.

Monetary wealth is relative, what is having too much? My idea of what I need may be greater than yours. So, to me, I may not be wealthy and to you I may be.

What is important is to share whatever wealth you have, it is for the less fortunate and it is in your giving and sharing that you will continue to manifest more and more. You will be an 'active account' for the Universe to flow through.

This one mantra helped me to shift the way I looked at money, receiving and giving it. I do not share this one easily, for I respect it so much and it can only work if it is instilled as a habit and is said with implicit trust and belief.

I decided that it was my right and duty to earn a living from what I enjoy and love doing. It is only through my earnings that I will, one day, be able to pay back all the angels who have helped me come this far and it is through my earnings that I can create more and more value for the people whose lives I have been blessed enough to touch.

So first, teach yourself some new lines around money. You can challenge the old beliefs so they hold no weight or logic, that will make it easier to alter them.

Money doesn't grow on trees. What if it did?

Money is filthy and dirty. Money is evil. All that = if I am poor, I am clean and good. Is this true?

Money is scarce. Is this true? Therefore if I want to acquire a lot, I am depriving others of it?

Money only comes from hard work, or artists have to struggle hard to earn a living. So if you love what you do, it can't be hard work and so you can't be rich? Is this true?

Spiritual people are not supposed to be rich. So, because I believe in the powers of The Universe and I feel a connection to Source, I have to be poor? Is this true?

If I'm successful, my friends will be jealous and stop liking me! How about if I am successful, I will inspire my friends to be successful, too?

Pink of Health Tips
All these choices and decisions require a nourished body and mind. Spiritually and physically. If there were three essentials that I feel fuel the magic of manifestation, they are: mindful drinking water, mindful exercise and mindful sleep. Get enough of them every day. If you are one who does not already have

some exercise in your life, commit now to exercise in some way tomorrow. Even if all you do is go for a thirty-minute walk around your block, do it.

Our society underrates sleep. Some people even go as far as saying they don't have enough time to sleep. When we try to burn both sides of the candle, and I remember how late I would stay up when writing this book, we are not giving ourselves the healing and processing that only sleep can provide. Sleep is essential and encompasses many elements of manifesting, which are, dreaming resting, allowing time, healing, spiritual connecting and cell restoration. Our emotional processing occurs mostly when we sleep.

Disempowering and unhealthy habits

You cannot get rid of a disempowering habit, what you can do is replace it. A habit is something you do at least a little bit of daily.

Habit: an acquired behaviour pattern regularly followed until it has become almost involuntary. Habits are routines of behaviour that repeat regularly and occur subconsciously. Habitual behaviour often goes unnoticed in people showing it, because a person does not need to engage in self-analysis when undertaking routine tasks.

Can you think of one health-habit that you know is disempowering and could be an obstacle to achieving the wellness that you want? It could be the common ones, overeating, smoking, taking recreational drugs, drinking too much, sitting on a couch all day. Notice, a habit is something that you are doing, as opposed to not doing, so there are many empowering habits that you could notice or add to your repertoire.

The good news is that if you can identify the habits that you believe will add to your well-being, you can use them to replace the unhealthy ones. For example a habit of drinking a lot of water, or drinking unsweetened herbal teas, exercise, breathing consciously, sleeping well and enough every night.

Mathematically speaking, we each have 24 hours in a day, what you do in those 24 hours will inevitably determine how your week turns out and then your month, your year, your life. It is like a bank account which will amass from the constant deposits. Once you make something a habit, it will become more automatic and subconscious, making it easy to practice. Have you ever taken vitamin supplements? Just as you need to take a tablet every single day to reap the benefits of the vitamin, the same goes with empowering habits: you need to practice them everyday.

The key to replacing habits is first to become clear, logically, about the reason and the feelings attached to the reason. When someone decides, for example, to quit smoking, by saying 'no' to smoking, they are saying 'yes' to a healthy lifestyle, better breath and to be a better influence on the people around them. When the reason becomes stronger than the desire and indulgence from the smoking, it will be easy to replace the habit.

Habits are neurological pathways we have etched in our subconscious and they become the habitual path we take without thinking. If you drive and always take the same route home, you will have noticed how, sometimes, even though you intended to go somewhere else, you automatically or 'habitually' took the road home without thinking.

When we give our minds new neurological pathways, we give ourselves choice. Then, when in the similar juncture, where the old habit would have normally kicked in, you will have choices, instead of the automatic reaction.

Sure, it will still feel easier to go the old way, but when you want to change something in your life, you have to first consciously choose the new way and, in time, this new way will become a habit.

How do we create new pathways? Doing things differently and repeatedly is the quick way to create new pathways for your brain to choose thus replacing bad habits. If you do not 'teach' your brain a new way, you will have no choice but always to go the old way. Habits put you on 'autopilot' continuously, to do things daily without giving them too much thought.

Anything we do again and again is a habit. So if we have more chosen desirable habits, we will live a life achieving more of our desires.

Imagine what life would be like, if you had some good habits in place?

For instance, having habits to walk every day, eat healthy food in every meal, meditate for a bit every day, swim every week, moisturise your skin and drink eight or more glasses of water and save a few cents daily, without having to think about doing any of them. Wouldn't that be wonderful? It would be like having an automatic savings account.

Things that we do everyday make up who we are and the results we have in our life. Bank accounts collect from constant deposits and good health is achieved or maintained from what we put into our bodies daily.

I believe it takes twenty-one days to form a new pattern but it can take up to ninety days to instil a habit. With initial discipline, you can create a new habit that needs little effort to keep. Habits can't be broken, they need to be replaced. We are always doing something, even when we want to 'not do' something. Choosing another thing to 'do' is the only way to change a habit.

Bad habits are bad because we are automatically doing something that does not serve our betterment. We do them all the time, without choice.

Anything done in moderation is not that bad, it is when we do them again and again that they can pile up to cause a negative, undesirable result.

So the first step is to identify the bad habits we have and decide why we think they are bad. Once you have decided which bad habits you want to rid yourself of, the next step is to come up with good habits you would like to instil.

Unless you have strong reasons to get rid of a bad habit, you are not going to do it. They have to be strong and personal reasons that fulfil your higher want. So the question here is, what do you want? If you want two opposite conflicts, it would be like planting poisonous weed in the same plot where you want to harvest a field of corn. Look back at the section on parts integration in Chapter 6 and decide which is the higher want.

Realise that your entire being wants you to be happy. Both sides of you, the side that feels like eating the chocolate every night and the one that wants to be slim, want the same for you on some level.

List all the benefits of making a change. Get books that show the benefits. Back this with facts. You have to convince yourself that replacing a habit has several gains or you will not stick to it. Research realistic information of the downsides of not making the change. If you can justify the bad habit to yourself, you won't want to give it up.

Now that you have identified the bad habit and the why, it is time to come up with new habits that will give you the similar feeling you get from the bad habit, take about the same amount of time and effort and will fulfil a higher want.

The thing that I have noticed about bad habits vs good ones is that bad habits often give us instant gratification and good ones take time and continuous practice to show any results. So be persistent and keep at the new habit, even if you feel you are not getting your desired results. The time will come when you will see the fruit of your determination and feel joy and satisfaction.

Devise a specific rule that will allow you to indulge in the 'bad' action on a rare occasion. Most things are not bad when isolated and done once in a blue moon, they are only bad when we let them become automatic and do them all the time without conscious choice. So, perhaps a plan to eat a small piece of a specific chocolate every Saturday night might be a good place to start. This will make it easier to choose the good habit daily, knowing that you have something to look forward to.

Declare your new habit to at least 5 people.

This will help you stick to it. The power of your word. Start taking your 'word' very, very seriously. Remember the chapter on declarations. If you say something, it is. Once you get into the habit of 'being your word' everything in your life will become more dependable. It is so, because you say so. When you commit to doing something, you will, because you don't want to ever break your word. When you declare your new habit to a few people around you, you will feel the added need to live up to it, because people are watching and you don't want to be a liar. It helps when someone else is holding you accountable.

Look at your home and work to ensure you do not have anything that will tempt you in the first thirty days. Remove junk food from your house and throw out the cigarettes so you won't need to struggle with willpower later. Even talking to someone everyday who makes you feel bad after hanging up could be a bad habit, so delete his or her number if you can.

Make it easy to choose the new habit. If it is to go for a walk, make sure you have your walking shoes with you all the time. Buy an extra pair to leave in your car or in your office, so you never have an excuse. Make it easy and try to predict the possible roadblocks or excuses you may want to use to not do it and prepare for them.

We are weakest at the point of making the choice, but when we 'pre-choose' we make it easier for ourselves at the moment of weakness.

For example, if you don't want to drink alcohol when you go out, offer to be the driver for the night; that way, you will have to be responsible as you have people depending on you who will hold you accountable.

Habits can take time to form. So meanwhile, stop and consciously think about your vision, what you want and then choose the action that will bring you closer to it.

Be patient, as the choosing will not be automatic instantly. It gets easier and easier and, before you know it, choosing the choice that is more conducive to you, having what you want in life, will become unconscious.

Do not judge yourself if you slip. Treat this time as a test. There is no failure, just results, so if you find the replacement habit you have chosen does not work well enough for you, choose a new one.

If you give up something for someone else, you may become resentful and you will always feel like you are sacrificing something. We have all heard of the reformed drinker or smoker who restarted as soon as the relationship ended. There is nothing wrong with being inspired by someone you care about to change your ways, but only do it if you believe in it. Do not worry about all that you 'should' have as habits. Instead choose your habits towards your health goals. Identify those wants and cultivate habits that, with time, will surely and truly manifest health in your life.

Drink water consciously, be grateful and imagine the water going in and plumping up every one of your cells. The mistake we often make is to isolate our thoughts, feelings and desires from our bodies. We treat them as separate entities, whereas to be an active manifester, we have to embrace our bodies as a field of attracting and expressing. Be grateful for each sip of clean water that you have readily available to you and think of those who don't.

Malti's 31-Day Habit Forming Checklist
This will act as a checklist to help you stay on track. This is just an example of how you will design it. If you are savvy with Excel on your computer, you can easily create a worksheet, you can download it from my website and then edit it to your liking, you could also just draw it on pieces of paper. Start it now, listing your Wealth and Health Habits and make it a habit. You can add more habits to the list. The purpose of this checklist is so you can tick in colour, every single day, that you do the empowering habit and cross in a different colour the days that you do not perform the habit.

As you know, it is what you do every day that will gather. Just as you take a vitamin supplement daily for it to have an effect, the same goes with empowering habits, just as if you were to put 1 coin in a jar every day, by the end of the month, you will have at least 28 coins. As with the Vitamin Supplement example, missing out one day and taking two tablets the next day will not work, as all excess vitamins automatically flush out from our system. Similarly, not walking one day and then walking for two hours the next may not be healthy for you. So please be sensible and be kind to yourself. Do not punish yourself, just be aware of your results.

The second and more empowering purpose of this checklist is that you can see with your own eyes how it fills up and the joy and sense of achievement of having more ticks in it than crosses will give you a true picture of how well you are doing. When you have desires that take time to manifest, the process may feel like you are not getting anywhere. Picture a baby who is lying on his tummy on the bed just learning to wiggle his body enough to move forward, and picture a toy rattle that is placed a few feet away from him; imagine how the poor kid would feel if every time he expended all the energy he had and got close to the toy, you pushed the toy further away. Similarly, not being able to see how far you have come can be disheartening. The checklist is designed to enable you to see your progress even before the desire manifests fully.

The sample of my checklist spreads across the following two pages. What we do everyday adds up to the SUM TOTAL of the results we have in our lives You can also download it from my website: http://www.multi-coaching.com

31-Day Habit Forming Checklist - http://www.multi-coaching.com

What we do everyday adds up to the SUM TOTAL of the results we have in our lives

Date	Date						
Day	Day	Mon	Tue	Wed	Thu	Fri	Sat	Sun
Walk 60 minutes		✓	✓	✓	✓	✓	✗	✓
Write in my TAG gratitude journal		✓	✓	✓	✓	✓	✓	✓
Drink 3 litres of water		✓	✓	✓	✓	✓	✗	✓
Listen or Dance to song from my Happy Play List		✓	✓	✓	✓	✓	✓	✓
Ask myself what's great about a situation		✓	✓	✓	✓	✓	✓	✓
Indulge in something from my Pleasure List		✓	✓	✓	✓	✓	✓	✓
Do something nice for someone		✓	✓	✓	✓	✓	✓	✓
Look at vision board		✓	✓	✓	✓	✓	✗	✓

Habit								
Say No to Something or someone and notice what you are saying Yes to		✓	✓	✓	✓	✓	✓	✓
Practice Plugging In	✓	✓	✓	✓	✓	✓	✓	✓
Say your personal declaration in a Plugged In state	✓	✓	✓	✓	✓	✓	✗	✓
Practice the body of Gratitude	✓	✓	✓	✓	✓	✓	✗	✓
Eat healthy midnight snack	✓	✗	—	—	✗	✗	✗	✓
Pilates or Yoga 4 times a week	✓	—	✓	✓	✓	✓	—	—
Drink less than 2 glasses of wine		—	✗	✓	✓	✓	✗	—
Show Love to someone	✓	✓	✓	✓	✓	✓	✓	✓
Insert empowering habit here								
Insert empowering habit here								
Insert empowering habit here								
Insert empowering habit here								

Exercising

Since I was a kid, every time I fell sick and went to see a doctor, he would ask my mother to get me to exercise. I had allergic colds often, he said exercise, I had fainting spells, he said exercise, I had stomach upsets and he said exercise. I was an obese kid so, to me, exercise was last on my agenda, you would catch me dead in my sports gear in school. I became the expert on making up excuses to the physical fitness teacher, to get out of physical training. When I grew up, got married and became pregnant the obstetrician said, exercise; then after she was born, they said exercise; now that I am in my forties and have so many exciting years to look forward to with osteoporosis, menopause, Alzheimer's, diabetes and God knows what else, again they say exercise. When my daughter was underweight, they said exercise. When my mother went through a nerve condition, they said exercise. It is not a conspiracy, I promise. So finally when I was 37, I took heed and I started to incorporate exercise into my life. I did not do it for a short period of time, I committed to a lifestyle that included exercise just as it included sleeping and drinking water.

Personally, I do Pilates and to me it is a form of meditation. I usually close my eyes and connect with the part of my body that I am working. In fact with Pilates it is even easier to do so, because with the breathing and focus needed on the core and pelvic floor muscles throughout, you can't help but be mindful and focus not only your energy but your thoughts to maintaining your core engaged and thinking of the other specific body parts or muscle groups you are working. This also became the only hours in the day when my phone would switch-off.

I used to practice this 'meditation' when I was walking as well; whether on a treadmill or on a path, I foresaw fat melting away from my body. I 'saw' myself shedding excess weight as I walked.

When you think about your body and your breathing you are instantly coming into the present moment. You are then able to experience the flow of energy. Become aware of your own breathing, the rise and fall of your chest, expanding ribs, your stomach muscles contract, your pelvic floor muscles clench and release, wiggle your toes and fingers, shrug your shoulders, all being aware.

Anything that involves your body, your mind and your breathing is essential to being healthy. Yoga and Pilates I think are fabulous ways to connect the three simultaneously and reap true benefits.

When I wanted to lose weight, I walked for 60 minutes a day and I did weight training for 45 minutes a day, I did this 6 days a week without fail. So depending on your goal, there are different options you can take. Now that I do not want to lose any more weight, I do Pilates four times a week and cardio three times only.

Get clear on the results you want to achieve from your exercise routine, go back to your jigsaw puzzle visualisation, if changing your body shape is one of your desires, only then can you make a call.

Our bodies are made to move and if you are seated at an office desk all day, or you are running errands all day with your phone ringing or beeping incessantly, you need to find an hour a day to connect with your body in exercise. The manifesting that occurs when you connect with your body is amazing. Plugging In is about your entire body, your thoughts and your feelings, not just your head.

Think about it as engaging your body into your desires, turning your entire body into a tower that attracts, like an antenna.

Weight

When you want to lose weight, you have to live and start behaving the way slim people do. I have read in countless books how we should emulate successful people to become successful. Why reinvent the wheel?

Do you have beliefs around your weight? 'I am over forty, so I have no chance', 'It is in my genes', 'I am already married and have kids, so what if I am fat'?

Well, if you believe these statements then they will be true for you. Look for evidence to back these statements and look for proof that these statements may not be true. Choose what you want to believe and, based on that, you will be able to move forward.

You can't do what you always did to get a different result. I used to be overconfident, thinking I could eat what I liked and not exercise and still have the body I coveted. Seeing the kilos pile on and my clothes getting tighter to the point of having to go up a size, I realised that I had to change my strategy.

Start watching what your slimmer and healthier friends do, walk in their shadow, shop for groceries like a slim person does. Walk the way slim people do, buy gym clothes and sneakers, even though you are not sure what exercise you are going to do. Act the part. Fake it before you make it. Behave and look like a slim and healthy person to become one yourself.

I had always been the biggest couch potato. Sitting in front of the TV with a bag of salt and vinegar chips and a glass of wine. In my school report cards, they declared me 'Obese'. But something happened, I decided one day that I wanted to drop a size in 8 weeks and I did it.

I performed the NLP technique 'parts-integration' (Chapter 6) where I could establish congruency between all my 'parts'. Without meaning to trivialise the issue, I used to feel that I had conflicting parts. A part of me wanted to eat like a glutton and another part of me wanted to be slim. Through Parts Integration, I could merge the parts in the knowledge that all parts of me wanted the same for me – joy and peace.

Then came the bigger question: what would give me that peace? The eating was only going to give me momentary gratification or pleasure, while the dropping a dress size hooked to so many other feelings of well-being and joy.

I knew that achieving that would help me feel more confident and look better. I know that much of my daily frustration lay in trying to select something to wear twice a day and then looking at myself in the mirror, breathing my tummy in and still feeling upset at the way I looked. I would have to change several times till I found something that looked the least fattening. Just the thought of being able to get rid of this frustration was enough of a motivation for me. And I started to picture myself in 'slim clothes' and looking great. The vision I had of myself in my mind's eye was like a magnet for me. The instant I decided, everything that used to seem so difficult and tiresome became so easy to do. Soon after, shopping and cooking healthy for myself and committing time everyday to exercise became a habit. I started thinking, acting and being slim.

Sickness, Illness, Pain

Whenever you focus on your sickness you give it all the more energy to grow, when you focus on your life you give yourself that more reason to thrive. Just like being in a dark room, you will only be able to see what you shine your torch on.

I don't mean to trivialise any illness or pain, so do what you have to do to get better, medically, and then get on with your life using all the life force you do have. Think of a body with illness as already being weak and having limited resources, you now have choice, if you wipe out all that little energy on feeling sorry for yourself and feeling the illness and the pain, you will exhaust yourself and all you are doing is feeding it more power.

Rest, be kind to yourself and as quickly as you can return to where you were before the illness, what you were doing; what was the centre of your focus before you fell ill? If that is not exciting enough then find something that is and devote your energies to that. Yes I am in pain and despite that I am going to focus on my work, my daughter, my life, my friends. Anything. Focus out with your energy, keep giving and doing and internally love yourself.

Sickness and ill health may visit you, don't allow it to take over your life. I have met people with breast cancer and Multiple Sclerosis and Fibromyalgia and Trigeminal Neuralgia and Liver Cirrhosis and Diabetes and it was all in their attitude that determined where the illness took them. Some ended with depression and got more sick and some went through, and still go through, treatment. The illness is just a part of them but does not consume them. I have had countless clients who had severe pain which paralysed them and then they focused on the rest of their lives, learnt to manage and live with the pain and, magically, the pain disappeared. When they focused out and became of use and contributed to society and the people around them, their pain disappeared and their health improved.

I read somewhere that the only difference between Illness and Wellness is the 'I' and the 'We', When you only think of yourself, 'I', you are victimising yourself and you are blaming yourself and you are 'feeding' the illness, whereas when you look at yourself as a part of this Universe and you do your part in giving and contributing in whatever ways you know, you focus on the 'We' and you experience Wellness.

Develop healthy and wealthy habits. You can download the Monthly Habit Forming Checklist to help you from the website. There is a sample of it at the end of the book.

'It's supposed to be a secret, but I'll tell you anyway.
We doctors do nothing.
We only help and encourage the doctor within'

— *Albert Schweitzer, German Alsatian theologian,*
musician, philosopher, and physician (M.D.)

Thinking Pink Tips on Health & Wealth

\# Be grateful for being human and affording enough to buy a book.

\# Be grateful for your meals and the basic needs that you don't have to worry about.

\# Give, give, give.

\# Create the vision board and flow out list.

\# This is a list of what you will do with the money.

List all the material possessions you desire, how you want to invest your money, who you will give money to, what you will buy and how you will share it. You can add images to this document and merge it into a vision board or you can do them separately.

Think of the experience, not money.
Exercise, sleep, drink water and shed extra weight.
Design your personal Monthly Habit-Forming Checklist.

II

Gratitude

Gratitude is not only the greatest of the virtues but the parent of all others.

— *Cicero*

Do you realise that you are already appreciating and you are already grateful? By saying that you 'like' something, you are appreciating it. Liking is the simplest form of appreciation. Do you recognise that being aware of what is around you is gratitude in action?

When you notice a smile starting to beam on your own face, you are filled with a certain joy and appreciation for the stimulus—the thing that made you smile. That is thankfulness.

Anything that makes you say 'Oh my God' is gratitude. You are noticing something as if it is the first time you are seeing it. When was the last time you looked into a little child's big eyes when they are excited and full of wonder and marvelled at what you saw? That is true gratitude. When was the last time you noticed the nature that abounds you, trees, birds, clouds, stars, the moon, waves? When was the last time you truly looked at people's faces and saw them smile?

We use words like 'thankfulness', 'appreciation' and 'gratitude', but the magic is revealed and activated when we *feel* them. And the simplest way to know you are grateful and thankful is when you *feel* the liking and the appreciation for that thing.

When you enjoy a song or a taste and you smile, when you greet someone and you feel that joy of seeing them, when you acknowledge someone's writing or art, when you read something that makes your face light up, *all* that is appreciation. I have had clients ask me, 'How should I practice gratitude? How do I feel appreciation? I am not sure how to do this?'

You are doing it all day, every day naturally, the only difference is to 'notice' and 'tag' it as thankfulness and appreciation when you do it. Truly say *Thank U* (U as in Universe here) for all you already have. By the way, the acronym TAG stands for Thankfulness, Appreciation and Gratitude.

Wonder, awe, marvel...saying 'wow' and even just clicking on 'Like', these are all simply appreciation and gratitude. So it is not something you need to learn, but just realise. Be awake and aware for all that is, all that already exists in your life.

If you are still unsure about how to practice gratitude, think of a child who has just seen his first ball and the wonder that he feels, or when a child learns to take her first step. I still remember my daughter's first few steps and the absolute joy in her face at the discovery as she walked to me; that is wonder and awe. If you are able to start noticing everything in your world as if you are seeing it for the first time again, you will be awed, too.

Practicing gratitude is one of the easiest ways to experience joy and happiness. Especially when you are feeling down and sorry for yourself and look around, saying that there is nothing to be grateful for, no one cares and no one has ever done anything for you. This is when you can stop and ask yourself a few questions; go back to your childhood and be grateful to your parents for giving you a life, feeding and nurturing you; to your siblings and friends for playing with you; to your teachers for showing you new things you never knew existed, offering you feedback to improve your skills; today to the methods with which you communicate and travel, like mobile phones, smart phones, social media and Skype; to the passionate geniuses like the founders of Facebook and Google; to the people who help put the food on your table and keep your space clean and throw our your trash.

I have neighbours in the next building who I am so grateful to. One is a family of Hindu priests and every morning they sing in devotion. And another family with two teenaged kids who, without fail every evening, blast the top 20 hits on their illegally loud and heavy-based sound system. I moved to India to enjoy the sights and sounds as I saw them in the movies growing up, and now I have it on demand like clockwork. How can I complain about it instead of being grateful?

Pick up the papers and, in one day, you will read about someone dying at the train track or several people perishing in a fire or people losing their homes to earthquakes and other disasters, you will read about bread-winners dying and leaving their families behind who don't even have the luxury to mourn or grieve their loss because they have to think about how to survive. The fact that you are probably sitting comfortably with this book in your hand says so much about what you have to be grateful for.

Yes, it is easy to be grateful when things seem to be going well. Practice being grateful for even the challenges in your life, look for what is still good and what you still have even when things seem terribly bleak. I look back at the relationships and people I have met, who have taught me so much about who I am and what I want and don't want.

On that note, I have been writing in my Gratitude Journal for years and, every single day, I have more and more to be grateful for.

Everything I want and need makes its way to me. At the risk of sounding like a nagging mum telling her children to eat their veggies, because she knows that they are good for them, start writing in the journal every night and get all the people you love to do the same, too. It does work and I want you to experience what I know you will. There is immense power in words...and putting your appreciation for someone or something into words that are expressed can change your life. (Excerpt taken from my foreword in *Thankfulness Appreciation Gratitude—My Journal*)

Writing in gratitude is just one way, though in my opinion it is a remarkably powerful and effective way, to feel gratitude, but the writing is not just about recording that you are grateful; it is simply a tool to help you feel and be aware of things to be grateful for all day.

I often give clients who sign up for my program a copy of *TAG—The Journal* as part of their start-up pack, to encourage them to write in gratitude every night. So I asked some of them and some of the members on the Facebook group for TAG, who diligently practiced this ritual, what it has done for them. Here are some of their comments:

The more I write how grateful I am for my wonderful family, the more reasons I have to be grateful :)

***

Writing in the gratitude journal raises my vibration. It keeps me in a space of abundance and thinking of expansion. Its makes me realise how fortunate I am for all that I have in my life.

***

I never realised that appreciating even the simplest things in life can bring so much joy, till I wrote them down daily in appreciation.

***

Writing in the gratitude journal is empowering because when I focus on the abundance of good things in my life it grows. And of course there's a huge shift in perspective and how we see our life.

***

I have been practicing writing in the journal of gratitude for almost 45 days and I have started appreciating lots of stuff in my life on a regular basis, which used to go unnoticed. I feel thankful to every good thing that happens to me, which might be very small in nature. I feel I have started receiving more abundance. Sleeping after writing in the journal makes me have a sound and positive sleep. Before writing the journal, I was almost hitting the phase of depression, but when I started appreciating and thanking for things in my life, situations did change, I started enjoying things around and helping myself big time to live high and happy. I am a much more evolved, content, composed and happy guy. So, yes, this journal has definitely been one of the things that was a major help in getting my life in control and moving towards enjoying in abundance. I also practiced writing in the journal early in the morning and it was phenomenal and brings in a separate energy all together to perform effectively during the day.

***

They say, God is in the details. But it's for us to recognise, enjoy and be grateful for these smaller (and quite often substantial) details that make our lives so wonderful. Malti's journal helped me see and appreciate the multiple joys that come my way everyday, ensuring that even when I'm down, there is always something that makes me happy and excited for the next day.

***

Being Grateful makes me realise the value of the little things in life without taking anything for granted. It converts the smallest of things into huge joys of contentment and satisfaction. After all this is so true - 'Oh contentment make me rich, for without thee there is no Wealth'! Being Grateful, fills me up with more positives, so problems seem minuscule.

***

Every quote I read in the gratitude journal connects me to my inner being. I read, reflect, ruminate & revel in the words.

***

As I write I feel more connected to my thoughts & feelings for each written word. I feel vast & boundless :)

The writing will support you but the goal is to become *a body of gratitude*. Awaken all your senses to feel joy and appreciation. Start by noticing. There is a huge tropical almond tree outside my apartment and in October, the leaves turn a bright orange, causing a whole different ambience to my view. That is gratitude! Listening and noticing every single thing that touches any of your senses and causes you to smile, that is gratitude! Now if you remember them and then at some point write them down, all you are doing is reliving the moments of gratefulness.

Receiving

Get over your reluctance to receive. It is in receiving that you are allowing the Universe and other people to love you and to give to you. When you feel gratitude you know that you have received. Your body and mind open up to the present and you are able to receive even more. Sometimes you are grateful for things that others do for you, or give you, and they are grateful that you allowed them to do so; by being open to receiving, you allowed them to give and that is necessary.

We are all giving and taking all the time, so we have to be willing to receive graciously as well as give more generously. In some cases, the receiving does not take anything away from the source and, in fact, just makes it even bigger. Think about being grateful when you see a rainbow; your noticing the rainbow gave it your love and appreciation. It is there for all to see and you being open to 'receiving' it did not strip any of the colour away from it.

Everything happens for a reason and so it is important to be grateful for any and every experience that we have, even when we are not sure at the time what the reason could be. I was blessed enough to meet His Holiness the Dalai Lama and Lama Zopa Rinpoche in Delhi recently, and because I was engaged to a follower of Bodhicitta who is very dear to them, I had the honour and blessings to have many conversations with Lama Zopa Rinpoche. I got personal blessings from both His Holiness and Lama Zopa Rinpoche on the launch of the *Thankfulness Appreciation Gratitude Journal*.

They presented my daughter and me with beautiful *Tara Thankas*, which are made of silk, to hang on my walls, saying to me that Buddha is happy with the work I am doing and blesses me to go forward and keep doing it. It was intense and I felt so humbled and blessed. A few months after the break-up, I realised how lucky I was when I heard stories of so many people who try to get close to His Holiness without much luck, whereas I was personally blessed. His Holiness also put his hand on the journal and gave me a white silk scarf to wrap around it. I started using that copy to write in in the start of 2012.

Learn to be comfortable while receiving gratitude from others. In some cultures when you say 'thank you' or 'I am so grateful to you', people are embarrassed and tell you not to thank them. I am still sometimes overcome with emotion when people express their gratitude to me and it often makes me cry. I am learning and practicing to feel the gratitude back towards them for giving me the opportunity to contribute to their lives. On occasions I thank them back for their trust, and on others I just say, '(It was my) Pleasure, treasure!' a phrase I learnt from my dearest friend Shauna Remen. And these are not just words, by saying these words you are saying that *it truly is a pleasure to be able to give* and this is why we have to be willing to receive, too.

It is OK to ask for help

Soon after my divorce, I went on a journey to discover myself. The journey led me to the experiential training I underwent, which then led me to training to become a life coach and writing my first ever published article, 'Marriages May End but Families are Forever'. I worked with a life coach myself at the time and I devoted weeks to research, asking experts, that I did not even know from halfway around the world, to contribute and together with their insights and my own reflection, I managed to put together those seventeen hundred words.

My ex-husband and I, though pretty young, had decided that we wanted to make our divorce work for the sake of our daughter. I decided to document what we practiced in this article which, in turn, was received with love and gratitude by its readers. When I was in school, one of my English teachers said something that made me believe that I did not have what it took to write well. This article discredited that old belief; as soon as it was published, it was translated into at least six different languages and posted all over websites internationally, it was printed and reprinted by various publications in Australia, Singapore, Malaysia, The Philippines, Hong Kong and India.

The sense of success and personal achievement I felt after that is what gave birth to my ability to churn out thousands of words a day, when inspired enough to do so. I realised that I had things to share that people wanted to read. I lost the need to 'hide' my truths and I wrote with honesty and I knew that it was OK to ask for help whenever I needed it and help always came.

I am grateful for my divorce, even though it was painful for all of us at the time. My divorce led to all the experiences I have had, that have brought me where I am today and I would not trade this for anyone else's place. I feel so blessed. All the opportunities I have had to ask for help have forged deep and true love and friendships in my life that would not have transpired otherwise.

I was at a ropes-course in one of the experiential workshop outward-bound sections that I was involved in and the object of the exercise was to form a human staircase in order to scale a wall to get to the other side. The intention was to get everyone to the other side. The group consisted of over a hundred men and women of all ages and sizes. The smaller ones had to go first, so I remember climbing on the shoulders of my friends and getting to the top, and up there, the trainer, and a few others were waiting to help. I struggled and tried hard to get up on my own and then my trainer, Mark, said specifically to me, 'You know Malti, it is OK to ask for help'. reaching his hand out for me to grab. He pulled me over and then I was able to help pull many of my teammates over, too. This was a huge lesson for me; sometimes our unwillingness to ask for help can be detrimental to the people around us, the people on our team.

Allow people to help you, accept a hug from a child and hug them back, practice saying thank you when people give to you and when the Universe showers on you, just by being. It is a cycle and we give and get, we may not always give back to the ones we take from, but we will give. Think of yourself as a pitcher overflowing like an endless waterfall, filling up and spilling over; we have to ask, we have to receive and then we experience thankfulness and we give.

Once a day, stop whatever you are doing and notice 2 things that you are grateful for in your situation or circumstance and in your physical space. Make a habit of this and truly expand your heart to receiving more to be grateful for. There is more than enough reason to feel grateful always; acknowledge that and where possible, give thanks for it.

When I write in my journal, I have noticed, it is not about recording events or situations, but rather it is for experiences brought to my world by the Universe, or a person who touched my life and made it that much better that day.

If you notice yourself mentioning a few names frequently, take the time to drop them a note and express that gratitude to them.

We have been so spoilt that we only ever notice what is there when it is missing. I am sure you have experienced that before. Have you experienced blackouts, do you suddenly become aware of all the gadgets and electrical equipments your day to day life is dependent on? When my Internet used to slow down even for a few moments, I became impatient and missed it so much, whereas when I had a good connection all day, I didn't even notice it, yet alone become grateful for it, and when the bill came at the end of the month, I used to get annoyed. Not anymore. Now, people laugh at me because I am grateful for my noisy neighbours and I look at paying my bills like an act of gratitude for the useful service it brought me all month.

Be as happy to give as you are to receive and always find reasons to be grateful. Gratitude is an attitude of asking yourself, *What am I truly grateful for in this situation? This is sensed and felt in the present moment and when a few things come to mind, you will be amazed at the intense emotion that flows with it.*

True manifestation is when you are grateful and you notice all that you have already manifested. I had that stark truth show up in my face late one night when I was about to fall asleep and I prayed—I was in one of my low moments of need—and in my prayer I asked for money, work, connections and a companion, then I went on to describe why I wanted all that just in the way I explained in the chapter on Plugging In – in sleep.

I prayed for a home, to be able to travel to see my daughter, to have opportunities to write more and be connected to more people I could give to and get from. I wanted money so I could eat well and have an opulent and abundant life. I prayed for a companion so that I could enjoy this abundance, intimacy and joy with. And then, as if like a brick being thrown at me, I realised that I was lying in my comfortable bed with my soft sheets and the temperature was perfect and I was just about to fly off to meet my daughter and that I had so many connections that I just needed to follow up on and I had a maid, Manda, who came in every day to cook something nutritious for me and that I rarely ate dinner alone and when I did, it was only because I wanted to, because I wanted to be with myself and to write or to watch an episode of my favourite TV show.

I already had everything that I was praying for! Tears of gratitude, humility and joy welled up in my eyes. The prayer was for the tomorrows that I feared might lack what I already have. Why did i even have to pray for tomorrow when today was absolutely perfect? We have everything we need already and we have hope and promises for everything we will need tomorrow. I was so loved and I had so much abundance and comfort around me and, yet, I was praying for love and money. Do you see the irony and the ungratefulness?

As soon as I realised this, I turned my prayer into gratitude and I turned my doubts and fears into trust. When you are not grateful for what you have, you send out missiles saying 'I don't want this that I have', I want something else, and this leads to a blockage in manifesting. When you are grateful for all that is already in your world and all that you already see coming in, you are saying 'Thank you, please send me more of this.'

Feeling grateful is the only vibration that the Universe will resonate with and it will send you more and more of its unlimited supply of all that you are already grateful for.

Thinking Pink Gratitude Exercises

Although the base is to feel it and feeling it is enough, just to support yourself in being able to experience it frequently, add some or all of these practices into your life.

Include your children or kids you know in some of these practices, to teach them early on.

1. Write in a *Thankfulness Appreciation Gratitude Journal* daily.

2. Schedule an outdoor walk and look at everything in nature and architecture and express in words your gratitude towards every little and big thing you see.

3. Feel gratitude when you eat and drink water.

4. Celebrate—A celebration is to mark and honour a happy event. When we acknowledge an event, an achievement or simply something that we are joyous about, coming together with others and celebrating it is also a form of gratitude. We are appreciating the past and the present and we are grateful. When we celebrate, we relish the present for all that it is, we are not concerned about the future; sometimes we look back and realise that a 'pat on the back' is in order and we raise our glasses in toast.

5. Look for something good in bad situations and feel the gratitude (Antagonist Exercise from Chapter 5). For example, if you injure your toe, be grateful that you can walk. If you have a car-accident, be grateful you have a car and that you are alive. There is always something to be grateful for, however bleak your situation or a particular incident may seem. It may seem challenging when you start but when you begin to see the joy and peace it brings to you, it will become second nature to you. Feel it in your heart and acknowledge it to someone, your gratitude will infuse and create more grateful people around.

12

The Beginning of the Rest of Your Life

Genuine beginnings begin within us, even when they are brought to our attention by external opportunities.

— *William Throsby Bridges*

Happiness is not a destination. You can't postpone it to when you have manifested all your desires and achieved all your goals or realised all your dreams; or maybe when you buy that home, or car, or when your kids are grownups, or your spouse retires, or you find that special guy or girl. Happiness is the little moments of joy you give yourself every single day, living a life in constant pursuit of happy and joyous moments. Happiness is love and the truest expression of love is gratitude. Happiness is moments of pleasure and happiness is laughter.

Spirituality is not the way we thought it was and is also not a higher place you get to. It is not a guru sitting on a mountaintop, giving up everything and living a life as a hermit. It is about tapping into the Universe and creating the lives we are meant to live, full of abundance, joy, love and laughter, with people around us. We all have our divine gifts within us. We all have our answers, we only need to tap in and connect to ourselves and unlock them.

What we seek is within and not without. Practice going in rather than always calling up someone when you need an answer. This takes practice, too. Stop asking people for advice, go in and see what comes up. Yes, for sure, ask experts for advice in their field, but asking friends and relatives what to do in your situation is futile. The more you look within for your answers and guidance, your internal compass, the better you will get at retrieving the data that you need.

If you have trouble getting there, trust that the search engine is a little slow sometimes and may require you to sleep on it. Literally.

You were manifesting before today and you are manifesting now. Every single thing that shows up in your world is because of a strong desire, whether conscious or not, that you have had. Even the people in your life that you would like to blame for your irritations and inability to practice manifesting are only vibrating your own thoughts and beliefs about them back to you. So look at the supplies and resources you do have and the love that is enveloping, you co-created this with the Universe, you will continue to create whether you like it or not, so choose your focus.

Someone asked God, 'If everything is already written in destiny, then what's the point of desiring and wishing?'

God smiled and said: 'Maybe I had written, "As you wish"'–Unknown.

In Chapter 12 of the Bhagwad Gita, 'The Yoga of Devotion', Krishna explains to Arjuna that the one who keeps doing their work, performing their life purpose and then renounces the attachment they may have to the fruit – he is the one who is dear to God. I have spent years working and persisting without questioning or doubting, I have had people suggest that I change my course or direction when they saw me struggling to make ends meet, but through the persistence and focusing on doing my own best and doing all that I can, then surrendering and allowing, I literally started to see the sprouts when I least expected them. Now I call myself the gardener, watering my plants.

Have I manifested all my desires? I have been manifesting again and again every day and I continue to do my work and when things get challenging, I practice Plugging In and I welcome immeasurable magic into my life, not just daily but moment to moment. Everything, every resource, every person with a resource that I need at a given time, shows up to me, offering exactly what I require. Every step of the way I see signs and I receive validation that people are benefiting, gaining value, manifesting their desires and that is enough to keep me working.

Trusting that everything is perfect and being grateful for every single thing has been what I persist at so much that it has become my habit. Do I get disappointed? Often. And then I look back and ask what was great about that situation and I come out grateful.

Lessons are age-old and available at our finger tips, but the learning happens when we are ready to master ourselves. It is so synchronised that as a child I used to play this game called Master Mind and it has only dawned in me, now, how significant the name of the game is and that I had the truth and the answers given to me then but I only see it now. I stumbled upon Napolean Hill's book, *Think and Grow Rich*, over twelve years ago, read it cover to cover but most of it went over my head. 'WHOOSH'. Then again in 2009, a friend gave me a copy highlighting the important messages, and again, I did not get it, and then finally in March 2011 another trusted friend suggested that I read it for the third time and insisted I finish it in a month and now I am a fan.

I will keep learning, as will you. I will keep doing, as will you, and I will continue to manifest the most beautiful experiences in my life, as will you. I will keep feeding my flow list and my vision boards will evolve, my jigsaw puzzle image will continue to upgrade and I am already grateful for all that is making its way to me.

So what to do now?

Trust that the world will be a better place and thousands of people will benefit from you manifesting your desires. Does everything happen for a reason or is everything just random and meaningless—which statement is more conducive to you in order to manifest your desires? I prefer to see that we are all connected, in giving and receiving, in relationships and in love and I know that by believing that through my hot air balloon flying off into the skies, other balloons will fly alongside me as well. As Marianne Williamson says so beautifully in her book *Return To Love* and then has been quoted in every personal transformation course, workshop and training I have attended:

'Our deepest fear is not that we are inadequate. Our deepest fear is that we are powerful beyond measure. It is our light, not our darkness that most frightens us. We ask ourselves, "Who am I to be brilliant, gorgeous, talented, fabulous?"

Actually, who are you not to be? You are a child of God. Your playing small does not serve the world. There is nothing enlightened about shrinking so that other people won't feel insecure around you. We are all meant to shine, as children do. We were born to make manifest the glory of God that is within us. It's not just in some of us; it's in everyone. And as we let our own light shine, we unconsciously give other people permission to do the same. As we are liberated from our own fear, our presence automatically liberates others.'

Know that as much as you try to uncover the truth, there still may be desires that you have not articulated or identified yourself and you will manifest those as well. Plug into source every single day and remind yourself to Plug In again if you feel that the connection is low. Live and decide by your values and your personal declaration. Let go of people, regrets, habits and things that no longer serve you.

I am still looking to connect the dots between compassion, gratitude, paying it forward, empathy, love and charity, I realise that I am looking for an opportunity to contribute to something meaningful. I recognise that all the work I have been doing with adults over the years, the experience from the thousands of hours of personalised life coaching that I have shared and all the exercises in this book, if they were shared with young children earlier on in their lives, the impact it would have on their experience would be awesome. If they learn to think from gratitude and take responsibility for their results from a young age, it would be world-changing. I am allowing the signs to appear, to guide me on.

Be patient and allow. Wait. Sleep. Rest. Take turns with the Universe. Do, allow, do, allow. Inhale, exhale. Know that all that you want is on its way to you, speeding towards you at Godspeed. Enjoy every moment, truly relish and savour the present. Love children, your own and others', be compassionate and put yourself in their shoes. Appreciate them as perfection, the way they are.

Share all that you are practicing with your kids and your friends. Helping other people feel good, have positive thoughts and feelings, and supporting them in manifesting their dreams will not keep your dreams any further; in fact the collective positive vibrations will bring them closer, faster.

Give to anyone and everyone you can, whatever you can. Give your time, your money, gifts, kind words, shelter, food, ideas, resources, help whenever you can, knowing that you will be the recipient of the same from someone else. Start at home, or near home, give a little extra to your helper, the security guard or watchman, the people who deliver stuff to you.

Aim for 10 per cent of your earnings but don't wait till you feel you can afford that; start with 1 per cent, which is easy, and commit to doing it daily. People will help you manifest your desires; unlike my analogies, your desires won't just fall out of the sky like rain onto your lap, though often it will feel like they did, but most of the time, someone else will be involved and instrumental in you getting closer to what you desire.

This is why it is so important to acknowledge all the love around you and the people in your world. Each new person you meet could be a random coincidence or the Universe playing out its plan so that you get to manifest your desires. When different people's desires match then they are serendipitously brought together from corners of the world to support each other and also help other hot air balloons take off. There is little that is new in this book, we all came into this world whole and loving beings, we all came in deserving, we just forgot along the way.

When I started to see coincidences in my life, I thought I had tapped into some supernatural power and called myself psychic for a while; then I realised that we all are intuitive and perceptive. When I met His Holiness the Dalai Lama and Lama Zopa Rinpoche and heard them speak on compassion, I found my own compassion, then I noticed that everyone around me was also compassionate and good.

You are also an instrument of the Universe, create pathways to flow love, money, energy, healing and all that you yourself want to manifest in your own life outwards to the people who come into your world with their cups extended. Fill them up. You are the 'use' of God's limitless opulence and supply. You don't have a glass that is half full or half empty, you have a bottomless jug to fill other cups with.

There is no destination; when you manifest the love, health, money you so desire and deserve, you will have the desire to manifest more. Your soul wants all these experiences and declaring your desires is just a way of directing you towards a pathway that will give you all the experiences you want on a deeper level. Fly up in your balloon, take your loved ones with you and while you are up there, make rainbows appear, just like I did.

Acknowledgements
A Few Pages From My TAG Journal

Don't Think of a Blue Ball was a three-year journey for me but most of it was written in six weeks.

My heartfelt appreciation goes to everyone who was with me over the past three years. First of all, to Ajay Mago, Dipa Chaudhuri and the entire team at Om Books International for believing in me and supporting me all the way with all my thoughts and ideas. To Nitin Abbey, for putting up with my thousands of questions and for extracting the 'gold' from me. Ram Kapoor, who painstakingly took time out of his busy moving schedule to offer me the invaluable feedback that he did. Throughout my life, my parents Lachman and Maya—you continued to give to me and nurture me, loving and believing in me with every decision that I made, giving me your unconditional love through it all, thank you.

My dearest darling daughter Drishti, who shows me everyday how much I am loved and how proud she is of me. She is my biggest blessing and I thank God for her every single day. You are the reason I live, I write, I am and I can't wait to read your first book. When you're in my arms... nothing matters.

My brothers, Sanjay for your guidance and reminding me who I am and Vishaal for your belief, continuous encouragement and teaching me so much through your own perseverance. Thank you both for always guiding me to go in.

My gorgeous and strong nephews, Nikhil and Krish and my beautiful niece Vania who love me just for being Bua Malti and always wanting me close; my sister-in-law and dear friend Reshma Bhojwani, for encouraging me to focus out, which is what sprouted my career, calling and purpose in life coaching.

My sweetest friend Priya Ratnani, for your unconditional love all through and for sharing some of my best and worst times with me, and Kiran Sekhon for always being there for me to say anything to, anytime of day or night, about anything at all.

My uncle Murli Bhojwani who gave and gave to me, without expecting anything in return, for nurturing Drishti like an angel whenever I could not be there myself. Aunty Laju for your home, inspiration, healing, your prayers and for being there for my baby, my three little Aussie brothers, Girish, Karan and Jai Bhojwani for believing in me and making me always feel that you were hanging on to my every word.

My uncle Sajan Bhojwani who has been like a silent angel, flying in, rescuing me and then always checking in on my well-being and progress.

For my family, Neel, Grace and Shenaz Nanwani for the love, respect and sense of belonging throughout the years and Simran Nanwani for always showing me her love and calling me *Chachi*.

My dearest friends, Suren Mirchandani for rescuing me when I was on the cliff and allowing me to fly higher than I ever have with grace, even before we had actually ever met.

Deepak Nagrani for your love, your presence and your care and concern throughout the years, always.

Sanjay Mirchandani for being a dream-weaver, for helping me with the chapter on Synchronicity and also your generosity and openness in sharing with me, even before we had met.

Ashok and Risha Vaswani for teaching me resilience and strength, and for all your love and help through the years, for believing in me.

Our darling Ashika Vaswani for her ethereal beauty that will always live in our hearts.

Harish and Roopa Fabiani, for your love and support even when I didn't believe in myself enough, for being a shoulder to cry on and a hand to hold.

Sunaina Gursahaney for being an angel and being there for me when I most needed it.

Chandru Bhojwani for helping me lift my game and believe that I could write and for all the music you brought to my life. ('Fly To Me')

Sascha Sippy for the magic carpet ride, introducing me to Buddhism and to Om Books, making this book possible.

My sister Reshma Shah for always bearing gifts and for connecting me to Diana and myself.

Diana Cooper for your mantras, Umesh Nandwani for seeing my wings way back when I had no clue.

Babita Bharwani for starting me out on the journey of personal development in 1999.

Toral Patel for your belief in me and for showing me manifestation in action. Sonal Singh for all your faith, trust and encouragement.

Shameem Samtani and Avinash and Ayaan Jashnani and Shantihi for your couch, your love, generosity and friendship through my darkest and then craziest times, for allowing me to be and never judging or criticising, for always having faith in my decisions and then for always celebrating with me. Thank you so much, guys!

Shauna and Yaron Remen for your trust, love and faith in me, for being with me through my transitions and growth always showing me your generosity, sharing your wisdom and above all setting a benchmark of what love, intimacy and a supportive family should look like.

Fay Fain for keeping me nourished, Natasha Lodhia for your friendship, love and for keeping me balanced, for being a sister to me.

Samir Purohit, Shirish Rajwade and Ketan Pathak at The Pilates Studio for keeping me fit through this time.

Sabah Shaikh & Mansi Shah at PINC for all your faith in me. Varun Bubber, Sasha Gusain and Kevin Lobo and Anupam Mittal for allowing me so many angles to express myself.

Kainaz Mehta for reintroducing me to myself and to Nealle Donald Walsch when I had forgotten Love and Fear.

Mark Hemstedt, The Works and Newfield Network for your love, all your coaching and for saying it like it is. Your guidance and telling me it is OK to ask for help through the years and then showing me I could fly up high in a hot air balloon and also find my centre before jumping off poles.

Christopher Howard for teaching me NLP and showing me the light.

Matthew Byrne for all that you showed me in the mirror and reintroducing me to Napolean Hill.

Our late Snoopy Bhojwani for showing me unconditional love. and care

Suzie Rughani for your edits and encouragement, Dipen Rughani for being my third brother.

My Bhojwani Goddesses, Nimrita and Bharti, all my sisters and aunts, for all your strength and love. Kiran Daswani for mirroring back to me confidence and self love.

My personal dream interpreter and friend, Simran Melwani for showing me the magic of my dreams, 'let's yin&yang till infinity and beyond'. Anuj Sharma for your beautiful designs and always having me look flowy and glamorous.

Sagar Mirpuri for your unfailing care, Renu Kirpalani for your friendship and faith. Rita Benjamin-Super and Rose Benjamin for your unwavering friendship through time and distance, Zeena Ahmed, Poonam (Miss India) Chandiramani and Loreeza Ali Bahaudeen, Prasanna Bhat and Shanel Chellaram for your love and well wishes in everything I have endeavoured. Belal Breaga Bakth, Roshan (Rima) Tulsiani, Shireen Melvani for all your quiet love and faith, Darshan Dave for exuding Tao calmness and for the dips whilst maintaining axes, for checking in on me as I hibernated with my edits. Katrina Kavvalos for reminding me to connect and relate. Cyrus Dubash for your tech support and friendship, all day any day without you this book would have been lost in MacWorld. Akash Loungani for helping me restore Mac at wee hours, for suggesting superlatives, for keeping me smiling and all that Jazz. Sushi Chanrai for your undeniable love and faith. Rohit Sood and Yogesh Jain for cheering me on at every step, Anjali Gvalani, Reshma Kalwani for your encouragement and well wishes always.

David Willey for taking the time to carefully explain the physics behind the bulb and tile demonstration and allowing me to quote you in reference to walking on coals.

My supportive study group, Lina Sutton, Miranda Yen, Simon Lau, Atul Jog and Samantha Xu who cheered me on and encouraged me as I took it all on at the same time. My amazing learning group, Bharti Bhojwani, Anjali Shahani, Shaan Shahani, Reemma Dalal, Neeti Mehra and Jemma Jadwani Antia and Seema Motiani for your commitment, openness and honesty to my learning.

Julio Ollala who re-affirmed my beliefs, Josephina Santiago for seeing me and teaching me movement, and Chris Balsley for teaching me resolve, my coach Deanne Prymek and mentor Lars Van Tuin at Newfield Network.

Lord Shiva, Lord Ganesh and Goddess Parvati and Archangel Gabriel, for guiding me.

All my clients who I cannot name and Facebook fans who contributed so much encouragement and wealth to this book and thank you to all the other amazing people in my life, you know who you are.

ALSO AVAILABLE

The Kept Woman and Other Stories (978-93-80069-27-2)
Kamala Das
"I feel a woman is most attractive when she surrenders to her man. She is incomplete without a man," averred Kamala Das shortly before her death in May, 2009. *The Kept Woman and Other Stories* explores the man-woman relationship in all its dimensions. Deprived, depraved, mysterious, mystical and exalted, each character culled from experience and observation, is an incisive study of love, lust and longing.

The last collection of writings that Kamala Das compiled herself before her death, *The Kept Woman and Other Stories* is a moving and compelling read.
Short Stories # Paperback # 192 pages # ₹ 195

The Company RED (978-93-80070-21-6)
Shantanu Dhar
Soon a major motion picture
A frightful and thought-provoking tale of hunts, *The Company RED* is the first novel of the RED trilogy by Shantanu Dhar.

A truly contemporary thriller! A must-read!

—Anil Kapoor
Fiction/Thriller # Paperback # 192 pages # ₹ 195

Three Sisters (978-93-80070-55-1) *Man Asian Literary Award, 2010*
Bi Feiyu

From the petty treachery of the village to the slogans of the Cultural Revolution and the harried pace of city life, three sisters strive to change the course of their destinies in a China that does not truly belong to them.

Yumi, the eldest, struggles to retain dignity as her ideal marriage falters. Yuxiu relies on her talent for seduction. And, Yuyang, the youngest, lays her hope in her own intelligence, securing the education that her sisters were denied.

A breathtaking and moving account of the challenges facing women in Communist China.

Fiction # Paperback # 310 pages # ₹ 295

The Eye of the Gods, 2012: An Awakening of the Conscience (978-93-80070-58-2)
Grazietta Salcedo D'Crescenzo

According to the Mayan calendar, 2012 is the year when humanity will witness great changes. These changes, it has been assumed, will be catastrophic but Mayan sources speak of a transition that will take place to a more spiritual way of being. *The Eye of the Gods, 2012: An Awakening of the Conscience* is a first-person account of Ah Ak'tun, born to Mayan parents in the Mayan region of Tikal, Mexico in AD 673. After the death of his father he is adopted by a venerable high priest who nurtures him to be his successor and weans him in the ways of the ancient Mayas and their special relationship with nature. He teaches him the significance of belonging to a priestly class that is duty-bound to oversee the activities of governors, merchants and politicians during times of war and peace. Ah Ak'tun in turn recounts his tale, giving us special insight into the cosmology of an ancient people.

Fiction # Paperback # 375 pages # ₹ 250

Cry of the Giraffe (978-93-80069-48-7)
Judie Oron

Labelled outcastes by their Ethiopian neighbours because of their Jewish faith, 13-year-old Wuditu and her family make the arduous trek on foot to Sudan in the hope of being transported to Yerusalem and its promise of a better life. Instead, they are herded into a squalid refugee camp until the day soldiers round up Wuditu and scores of others, forcing them back to the Ethiopian border.

Throughout her harrowing trek across the scorching sand, and the humiliation, fear and despair she later faces as a slave, Wuditu's only hope is to be reunited with her family in Yerusalem.

Based on real events, this story mirrors the experience of thousands of Ethiopian Jews who fled from hatred, persecution and brutality to a new life in their spiritual homeland.

Fiction # Paperback # 232 pages # ₹ 195

Thunder Over Kandahar (978-93-80069-47-0)
Sharon E. McKay

Best friends Tamanna and Yasmine cannot believe their good fortune when a school is set up in their Afghan village; however, their dreams for the future are shattered when the Taliban burn down the school and threaten the teacher and students with death.

As Tamanna is faced with the prospect of an arranged marriage to an older man, and the Taliban target Yasmine's Western-educated family, the girls realise they must flee. Travelling through perilous mountain passes, the two unaccompanied teens find themselves in mortal danger as they confront land mines, a suicide bomber, and roving bands of the Taliban. But when the two girls are separated, they are left without the one thing that has helped them survive—each other.

Fiction # Paperback # 288 pages # ₹ 195

Delhi OMG! (978-93-80070-68-1)
Vinod Nair

Delhi OMG! traces the journey of Dinesh, a middle-class offspring as he meanders through life and the city of *Dilli* in his struggle for survival.

The journey takes him through the many signature spots in the city, exposing the underbelly and presenting a side which is rarely seen. The loss of innocence riddled with myriad splashes of contrasting, funny and often contradictory shades, this tale attempts to expose the superficiality that lies beneath, in a way that is shocking, real, hard-hitting and humorous.

Consumed as Delhiites are in their world of make-believe and maximising their returns, with each one trying to be what they are not, Dinesh discovers that the city allows one to revel in their belief of having actually succeeded.

But have they, really?

Welcome to Delhi ... as we think we know it!

Fiction # Paperback # 312 pages # ₹ 195

Two Mothers and Other Stories (978-93-81607-09-1)
Khalid Mohamed

Bravely personal with quantum leaps into the imagination, *Two Mothers and Other Stories* by film critic, scriptwriter, playwright and director, Khalid Mohamed, explores a variety of themes ranging from familial bonds, the lingering Indian royalty, and media stratagems to Mumbai's fast-vanishing Zoroastrian Irani cafés and the bold new world of website sexual relationships. Unfailingly entertaining, his first collection of stories presents what it is like to be immersed in life with its inexhaustible twists, shocks and surprises.

Fiction # Paperback # 264 pages # ₹ 295

Meet Me At The Border (978-93-81607-18-3)
Inder Raj Ahluwalia

Meet Me At The Border presents unforgettable vistas of nature that include the world's highest sand dunes just minutes away from endless beaches; the world's oldest desert; an exceptional variety of wildlife in sanctuaries that are role models in environment preservation; safaris that bond one with nature; a hotel made entirely from ice and snow; an underground hotel; service that's an effortless whisper; blazing sunsets melting into lantern-lit romance; cruises that are almost sinful in terms of what they offer; meals that are the envy of royalty; thermal springs that provide instant rejuvenation; festivals that border on the sublime; people who are still living in the past, and much more. A must-read!

Travel # Paperback # 272 pages # ₹ 295